PLAIN & FANCY

PLAIN

American Women and

Curious Works Press

& FANCY

Their Needlework, 1650-1850

Susan Burrows Swan

Austin

Plain and Fancy: American Women and Their
Needlework, 1650–1850

First edition published in 1977 by Rutledge Books

Revised edition published by Curious Works Press
107 RR 620 South, #11-E
Austin, Texas 78734

ISBN 0-9633331-3-5

All items illustrated are owned by the Henry Francis
du Pont Winterthur Museum unless otherwise
specified.

Photography by George J. Fistrovich unless otherwise
specified. Glossary illustrations by Carol Hines

Abbreviations used in the legends:
H = height W = width
DMMC, WM = Joseph Downs Manuscript and
Microfilm Collection, Henry Francis du Pont
Winterthur Museum Libraries

Plate 1. (half-title page) A hollow-cut American silhouette stamped by William Bache with additional hand painted hair and lace details. Boston; 1800–1815. Photograph by L. Delmar Swan. Author's collection.

Plate 2 (frontispiece). One of the most artistically drawn and executed Boston fishing lady pictures known. Unfortunately, it is unsigned. The tent-stitched canvas work is done in crewel and silk with accents of metallic threads. Each of the three groups of figures recur on other Boston-type pictures, alone or in combination. For a cluster of the most appealing dogs in needlework, see the detail of this picture, Figure 28. 1745–55. H. 21"; W. 42".

Plate 3 (right). A 1737 sampler in the earlier, long and narrow style by ten-year-old Jane Simons. It is uncommon to find an eighteenth-century sampler worked in crewel yarns, as this one is. Someone experimented with a few drawn work stitches in linen thread near one of the tulips. History of ownership in Oyster Bay, Long Island. H. 20 15/16"; W. 8 5/16".

Contents

Preface to 1995 Edition

THIS BOOK BEGAN years ago when I realized that needlework offered early American women their primary outlet for creative expression. Indeed, except for needlework, almost no tangible products made by the women of centuries past remain. It occurred to me that surviving needlework projects represent one of our few remaining links with one half of our ancestors.

My study started with the objects. In its own collections, Winterthur Museum possesses more than seven hundred pieces of American needlework made before 1865. By arranging these and other pieces according to techniques and dates, and by allowing for variations in individual abilities, I began to see a pattern in the development of the needle crafts in America. The finest work was done before 1785. Between 1785 and 1825, the work was proficient but not as masterful as earlier efforts. From 1825 to 1875, a marked deterioration in needlework skills became apparent.

In an effort to understand these trends, I turned to primary sources. Eighteenth- and nineteenth-century newspapers contain valuable data in the form of hundreds of advertisements by schools that list the kinds of training they offered young women. By charting these advertisements according to the needlework forms and stitches, academic subjects, and other accomplishments they referred to, and by correlating this information with locations and dates, I gained a more precise idea of what needlework was being done where during the three different periods. The Glossary contains much of this data.

Women's magazines of the eighteenth century offered a philosophy by and about women that helps to explain some of the changes in the needlework of the past. In particular, the inexpensive and widely read nineteenth-century magazines reveal a dramatic connection between women's lives and their needlework, if only in that these periodicals placed specific needlework instructions virtually side by side with columns of advice to women. Inventories and wills hold clues to the importance of possessions. Finally, private thoughts recorded in diaries, journals, letters, and recollections, as well as public pronouncements by ministers, editors, and "manner" books, reveal the emotional states and ideas of the day.

I realized that in these sources I had at best a representative sample of what only a select group of women were thinking. The limitations of this material are obvious: the women who were committing their personal feelings to diaries or recording their days' activities in journals comprised a small portion of the minority of women literate enough to keep such records. Women who wrote for publication—a daring act even in the more enlightened days of early American life—represented an even more exceptional few. And the role models urged upon women of the past, like role models today, represented no one at all. They were models, not real people.

Fortunately, the women who did decorative, or "fancy," needlework corresponded fairly closely to the women who read or produced this literature. These women, whom I have sometimes referred to here as "of the better sort," were usually but not always wealthy, relatively well-educated, and, most importantly, socially successful, or "genteel" to use a term that accomplished ladies favored to describe themselves. Moreover, particularly before 1800, the surviving fancy needlework tends to have been made in the same towns and cities from which we also have newspaper records. If we cannot gain a completely accurate picture of these women from the newspapers and magazines they read and from the diaries and journals a few of them left, we can make a more educated guess about them than about the housewives, far more numerous, who left behind no written records. As "plain" needleworkers, common housewives have a lesser part in this story. In quoting those who did express themselves in manuscript or print, I have preserved the original tone of that writing by retaining archaic spellings and grammatical forms as well as the use of italics.

This book has been titled *Plain and Fancy* because these common sewing terms summarize the lives of women as well as their needlework. But unlike the lives of early American women, there is more fancy than plain here. Fancy is of course more fun, not only for the women who did it, but for people today, such as myself, who enjoy needlework both for how it strikes us aesthetically and for what it tells us about the women who created it.

In organizing this book, I chose to keep the plain and the fancy—both women and their needlework—as separate as possible. Although the different segments of early American society shared many practices, customs, and beliefs, there were distinct divisions among them. For example, only the "middling" and "better sorts" of women could afford to do fancy needlework. Thus, the first chapter in the book, "Plain Sewing, Plain Housewives," covers a common denominator of women's lives and their sewing. The rest of the book is limited to the women who did fancy sewing. Chapter 2 traces the evolution in the education of young ladies, because the trends in education provide an excellent insight into the changes in needlework styles and the changing roles of women. The last three chapters explore the three basic eras of fancy needlework mentioned above: 1650–1785, 1785–1825, and 1825–1875.

I have discussed different needlework forms in these eras, mindful of the fact that inevitably there would be overlaps. For example, American women were quilting long before the nineteenth century, but I chose to examine quilting in the last chapter for reasons that will become clear there. Two centuries of American women and their needlework is a multifaceted subject, defying quick and easy structural breakdown. In an attempt such as this to determine not only how people lived, but what they thought and how they expressed their thoughts through their art, the most delicate matter of all is to dramatize change without overstating it. If I have established needlework in a historical context that is both accurate and clear, then I have succeeded.

THE RESEARCH FOR this project has often been most absorbing to me, and the transformation of the results into a book has been a great challenge. I have been exceptionally fortunate in encountering many people of very generous natures, both during the research, and in the writing and rewriting of this book. Colleagues at the Winterthur Museum, past and present, to whom I am especially grateful are: Nancy Goyne Evans, Arlene Palmer Schwind, Karol Schmiegel, Deborah Waters, Benno Forman, E. McSherry Fowble, Deborah Kraak, Linda Eaton, Kathleen MacIntire, Barbara Shellenberger, Frank Sommers, Eleanor Thompson, Page Talbot Gould, Robert Trent, June

Sprigg, Beatrice Taylor, Katherine McKenney, David Schuyler, David Kiehl, Alberta Brandt, Karin Bengston, Bill Steltzer, Gary Kulik, and Catherine Hutchins.

I am indebted to a number of kind and helpful friends, collectors, and scholars: Davida and Alvin Deutsch, Carol and Robert Baker, Jean and Joseph McFalls, Betty Ring, Joan Stevens, Polly Stocker, Sandra Downie, Ruth and Theodore Kapnek, and Frederick Weiser.

The Chester County Historical Society allowed me to include some of its superb collections in the illustrations. Mr. and Mrs. Philip Hanes, Jr. generously permitted me to publish the lovely Gilbert Stuart portrait of the young ladies doing tambour work.

George J. Fistrovich conceived the then innovative idea of photographing the objects to suggest their original settings. I appreciate his originality, artistry, and cooperation. I am also grateful to Dwight P. Lanmon, the Director and Chief Executive Officer of Winterthur Museum. To the people at Rutledge Books who contributed their very special talents to the original book, I express my deep gratitude: Jeanne McClow, Editor in Chief; Allan Mogel, Art Director; and especially Jeremy Friedlander, Editor, whose skill and creativity made the original book possible.

Kathleen Epstein proposed this new edition and allowed me to include many of the new examples and new research I acquired while Curator of Textiles at Winterthur. Kathy, an exceptional scholar in her own right, has handled all of the editing and technicalities of producing this new edition and has generously shared her own fine research, particularly of the seventeenth-century samplers and lace. She and her husband, Jerry, are brilliant and stimulating friends.

Most of all, I am indebted to my family and especially my husband, who has given me his help, support, and love for forty-four years.

How blest the Maid whose bosom no headstrong passion knows,
Her days in Joy she Passes, her nights in soft repose.

KEEP WITHIN COMPASS AND YOU SHALL BE SURE, TO AVOID MANY TROUBLES, WHICH OTHERS ENDURE; KEEP WITHIN COMPASS

KEEP WITHIN COMPASS

A Virtuous Woman is a Crown to her Husband.

ENTER NOT INTO THE WAY OF THE WICKED, AND GO NOT IN THE PATH OF EVIL MEN.

Introduction

Figure 1 (opposite and detail). A moralistic print entitled *Keep within Compass*, defining the boundaries women should observe in their lives and the consequences if they strayed beyond. Unsigned sepia engraving. United States or England, 1785–1800.

THROUGH THE YEARS in more affluent cultures, men have traditionally relegated women to playing decorative, seemingly subservient roles, and women have allowed this. Perhaps it made most women feel pampered, protected, freed from the pressures of coping. Except for some wonderful, rare rebels, whose words I shall quote in this book, it took until the mid-twentieth century for American women to demand and expect a more fully egalitarian society.

Nevertheless, some of our female ancestors were incredible women. From early on they were brave and able, often working beside their men, sharing responsibility, and building this country with their own hands. They bore children, buried children and husbands, and survived. On the frontier, they helped to clear the forests, work the fields, chop wood, build fences, and defend their homes and families. They tended children, grew vegetable gardens, made candles and soap, cooked, cared for livestock, and fished. A few exceptional women were painters, poets, and writers. A few even fought in war, marching with the armies and bearing arms. There were also skilled women: blacksmiths, printers, engravers, and silversmiths. They ran businesses, engaged in commerce, administered property.

Beyond and above all the things they did, they sewed. And they taught their daughters to sew. Their needlework took two forms: plain and fancy. Plain sewing included the essential forms of household needlework, namely, the cutting out and stitching of underwear, ordinary clothing, sheets, towels, and bed coverings. This work required simple stitches, among them back, whip, cross, and running. Knitting and the marking of household linens also fit into this category. All women had to do plain sewing, or make provisions to get it done.

Fancy needlework encompassed all the non utilitarian forms. Since by its very nature decorative work was superfluous, only women in comfortable financial circumstances enjoyed the leisure time that enabled them to indulge in it. Most surviving needlework artifacts are fancywork. This is not surprising for they were cherished mementos, passed down through generations, whereas plain work was consumed—used and reused, cut down and remodeled—until only the scraps remained, finally to be used in quilts.

This book's purpose is to show the integral part needlework played in the lives of these women, and particularly how it allowed them to express themselves in a male-dominated society. For needlework, in addition to being the most important contribution made by early American women to the decorative arts, was also their most acceptable outlet for creative expression and, indeed, in many instances the only concrete evidence of their endeavors. Needlework speaks to what it was like to be a woman in early America.

Throughout this period of history, it was the rare women, regardless of class, who escaped the basic requirements of her sex: marrying, bearing and rearing one's children, and taking care of a load of household chores, of which plain sewing was only one. This, the basic role of the common housewife, was the basic role of all women from 1650 to 1850. Even the stylish lady remained in essence a housewife and mother.

It was a life of unrelenting hardship for many women. Plain sewing occupied only a small part of the day, and it often came as a relief from the arduous drudgery that was their normal lot. To our eyes plain sewing seems an uninspired aspect of their lives. Yet it had to be done, and women got it done without question or complaint, just as they got married, had babies, and ran households. For women, plain sewing was an inescapable part of an inescapable lifestyle.

For the daughters of prosperous men, plain sewing had added significance: it was the essential first step in learning fancy needlework, a stylish lady's most important accomplishment. For the most part, a young lady went to school to cultivate the traits that would attract a husband. Fancy needlework was invariably a part of her education and often was the whole of it. Scholarly training added little since a cultivated intellect usually did not help a female either to attract a man or to serve him as his wife. Through the ups and downs of female education over this two-hundred-year period, one overriding theme remained: the subordination of a woman's mind to her duties as wife and mother. Even so enlightened an observer as Dr. Benjamin Rush, physician, statesman, and social commentator, who called for women to be "governed by reason," did not challenge the assumption that they should be obedient housewives and dutiful mothers.[1]

Society consistently failed to appreciate the intellectual capabilities of its women. Yet cultivating women's other qualities sometimes genuinely encouraged their self-expression and fulfillment. In the eighteenth century, before the Revolution, craftsmanship flourished in the colonies, and the women who did fancy needlework during this period must be considered on a par with the other fine craftsmen of the day.

These women, however, were still housewives, albeit well-to-do ones, who had to find time to do their fancywork while they ran their households. Legally they were wards of their husbands; socially they were adornments to them. Practically, however, they were nearly their equals. These women stayed home because they had to, to oversee the smooth functioning of their households. Others left the home because they had to, to assist their husbands in business and to take over those businesses when widowed. These were sober, resourceful, meticulous workers, in their fancy needlework and in their lives.

After the Revolution, the leisure class, which had begun to develop in the colonies as early as the first half of the eighteenth century, emerged in full flower. The women who belonged to it had tasted the eighteenth-century equivalent of the good life, and they wanted to keep it, even as they rebelled against many of the more confining strictures on women. These women no longer had the time or inclination for the precise, unassuming craftsmanship that had marked needlework done earlier in the century. In short, this was a time of rising expectations.

A few enlightened thinkers were advancing radically new suggestions for improving women's opportunities, but there was little change in women's substantive status. Even though the women of post-Revolution America were likely to have been more sophisticated and better educated than their predecessors, in general they remained ornaments to their husbands. If anything, the idea of woman-as-adornment grew stronger. In the nineteenth century, women became more securely ensconced in the home and lost many of the common, if unspoken, freedoms they had enjoyed earlier, in a less-structured society. The Victorian Age had descended.

In this, the final period discussed in this book, the exquisite fancy sewing of the eighteenth century, worked by young unmarried women, all but disappeared. In its place the uninspired copy stitching called Berlin work became fashionable, primarily for married women. As Victorian society and industrialism foreclosed any other options, most well-off women found themselves assigned to the home, rededicated to serving their families. They continued to work with their sewing needles almost as industriously as before, but the era of fine needlework had passed.

❦

In 1815, AN ICONOCLASTIC seventeen-year-old, Mehetable May Dawes of Massachusetts, reflected, "All men feel so grand and boast so much . . . about being lords of the world below . . . we are very willing men should *think* they govern since they are happier for so thinking while to ourselves we laugh at the deception."[2] The appearance of subservience was well maintained by fancy needlework. It allowed women to posture prettily and to create lovely articles. Feminine, delicate, and ornamental, it harked back to the docile scene of Penelope patiently weaving while waiting for the return of Ulysses.

Consider, for example, the engraving *Keep Within Compass*, published in the third quarter of the eighteenth century (figure 1). A well-dressed lady strolls serenely in a garden, using a knotting shuttle (see Glossary) while she walks; even at leisure she is industrious, her hands never idle. The compass is a symbol that openly acknowledges the rigid confines of her status. Only by obeying the rules could she become "A Virtuous Woman [who] is a Crown to her Husband." She is admonished to "Keep Within Compass And You Shall Be Sure to Avoid Many Troubles Which Others Endure."

To drive home the message, in the corner vignettes the engraver has depicted some of the pitfalls to which a woman of the times might fall prey. For example, she might take to drink (upper left) and neglect her child as she becomes addicted to card playing and gambling (upper right). This in turn might lead her to prostitution. In the third vignette (lower right) she is shown soliciting a man when a night watchman intervenes. And finally, the ultimate degradation: a hopeless life in prison (lower left).

Needlework, then, was well within the most restrictive compass of a woman's possibilities and a garnish to it. Indeed for many generations, handwork and fancy sewing epitomized the ideal woman. But there is more to the story. If fancy needlework was a symbol of a woman's way of life—and it was—that way of life was not always as rigidly confining as the puritanical exhortation *Keep Within Compass* suggests. In her needlework a woman was expressive and often creative. At these moments she gave us a revealing insight into her character and her times. These achievements help us to see some real and remarkable people beneath the cloak of domesticity and subservience, which for the most part has shrouded our perceptions of these women.

NOTES

1. Rush, "Thoughts upon Female Education," 292.
2. Diary of Mehetable May Dawes, June 21, 1815.

1 Plain Sewing, Plain Housewives

Figure 2 (opposite). Four examples of well-marked household linens worked in cross stitch, also called marking stitch. United States; 1800–25.

Every early american girl learned plain needlework, usually starting as soon as she could manipulate a needle. A girl from common circumstances certainly had to know how to sew because as a housewife she had to make and mend all the cloth products her family needed, not only clothing but bed linens and towels as well. A wealthy girl needed to know how to sew because it was unlikely that she could afford to pay someone else to do all the plain sewing her household required: more clothing, bed linens, and towels, plus curtains and table linens. She could delegate much of the work to servants or slaves, but she needed to know enough to direct them, and she might even have to teach them. Besides, without knowing the simple and basic techniques of plain sewing (figure 2) she could not begin to learn fancy needlework (see Glossary).

Plain sewing was so basic to a girl's training that any girl who could not sew was considered odd, certainly not ready for marriage. Marriage was not merely a goal in life for a girl; it was her mission. She heard enough derogatory remarks about spinsters (also known as "thorn-backs," "stale virgins," "antick virgins," "stale maids," "and old maids") and witnessed enough contemptuous treatment of them to understand very early that if she were to fail to marry, she would bring not only unhappiness but a measure of social disgrace on herself and her family. To win a husband and to serve him well, she had to know how to sew.

Moreover, plain sewing provided a woman who had little or no help in her household an opportunity to sit down for a while and let her mind wander, all the while secure in the knowledge that she was doing something productive, keeping her hands busy. This was an important consideration, for to be idle was thought to be sinful. As the Reverend Isaac Watts, author of *Divine Songs for Children,* a popular source of sampler verses, wrote, "Satan finds some mischief still for idle hands to do."

Plain sewing was a task that lent itself to socializing, too. A woman could bring it with her when she went out visiting, or she could pick it up while socializing at home. Because it required no great attention, she could join in the conversation or listen while someone else read aloud.

In itself, plain sewing could be either arduous and repetitive or relaxing and almost therapeutic, depending on the particular task and the needle woman's mood. The products of the work—fresh new sheets, pillowcases, linen towels, and chemises—could provide a woman with a great deal of satisfaction with her skill and her contribution to the household. For the woman who made her own outer clothing, the completion of a new or even a remade gown must have been an especially pleasurable event.

Before colonial women could do plain sewing, however, there had to be fabric with which to work. It is difficult for us in this industrial age to appreciate fully the value that was assigned to most textiles during the seventeenth and eighteenth centuries. They were, in fact, considered so important that inventories of household possessions listed them immediately after land holdings, money, and silver. Since repairing and reusing an article of clothing was far less costly and time-consuming than making it new, a garment was mended and remodeled over and over again until the fabric became so badly worn that it was cut down and remade into a garment for a younger, smaller member of the family. And when the smallest child had finally worn through it, it could be cut up and pieced together to make a bed quilt. Consequently, few examples of plain clothing survive in original condition today. Even the more elaborate garments we have from this time are nearly all remodeled versions of earlier costumes.

Several factors accounted for the high value of textiles. During colonial days, cotton was not the basic textile that it is today. Before the Revolution, most of the cotton that came to the colonies was grown in India and then shipped to England for processing, either as fiber or as cloth. Although cotton mills began operating in New England, New York, and New Jersey in the late 1780s, it was not until well into the early nineteenth century that Eli Whitney's cotton gin and Arkwright's mill solved the previous problems in spinning and weaving cotton. With the advent of this new technology, cotton yarn and fabrics became inexpensive and popular in the United States.

Silk fabrics were even rarer during the colonial period. Some families might grow their own mulberry trees and cultivate silkworms. However, the rest of the silk-making process required too much labor to support profitable large-scale commercial production. The process called for a silk reeler, who would unwind the fibers and twist them into thread. Then a weaver would turn the threads into fabric by means of special hand looms. One such craftsman, fringe-and-lace-maker James Butland, advertised in the August 15, 1774, issue of the *Pennsylvania Packet* that "any person having silk of their own may have it manufactured into . . . silk stockings, sewing silk, ribbons &c." After the Revolutionary War, American ships began regular voyages to China and brought back silk fabrics at steadily decreasing, though still not low, prices. By about 1830, the competition of foreign silk put the continually faltering American silk makers out of business.

Because both cotton and silk were considered luxury fabrics and were scarce during the colonial period, the primary clothing and household fabrics were made from linen or wool, both home grown and imported from England and Europe. Newspaper listings of fabrics for sale, not only wool and linen, but also cotton and silk, made up perhaps the greatest single category of newspaper advertisements. However, those people living in rural areas had to rely on home-produced yarn, which meant starting from scratch by raising flax for linen or sheep for wool.

The elementary steps involved in making fabrics were tedious, time-consuming, and in the case of home production mostly the province of women. Spinning was one such women's activity, often assigned to an unmarried daughter or another unmarried female relative living with the family or, in wealthier circles, to a servant or slave. Because this dreary and tiring task was usually assigned to an unmarried woman, the derogatory connotation of the word *spinster* evolved.

The type of spinning wheel that the spinster used depended on the type of fiber with which she was working. The wheel for wool was large and was turned by hand. Sometimes called a walking wheel, it required the woman to back away from the wheel while she spun the yarn and then move forward toward the wheel to wrap it onto the spindle. Obviously, producing yarn on a walking wheel could be wearisome. The wheel for flax was smaller and was operated by a treadle, so that a woman could work while sitting down (figure 3). Instead of having just a spindle, the flax wheel had a more sophisticated mechanism, known as a flyer, that automatically wound the yarn on the spindle after the turning wheel had imparted a twist to the thread.

Many women, however, used an even simpler device, the drop spindle, which has been common in primitive cultures for centuries and has produced yarns of the finest quality. This stick-like spindle, which relied on gravity to make it work, was weighted at one end with a disk, known as the whorl. To use the drop spindle, the spinster held a bundle of fibers and attached the end of one of these fibers to the spindle. She then twirled the spindle as she released or dropped it and continued to feed fibers to it until it reached the ground. Approximately one yard of thread could be spun on each drop of the spindle. Easily portable, the drop spindle proved a functional way for a woman to continue the task of spinning even while sitting outdoors or visiting with friends (figure 4).

Figure 3. Sketches of a flax spinning wheel (far left) and clock reel (far right) by John Lewis Krimmel. Detail in lower left corner shows the flyer mechanism. United States; probably 1819. *From the Krimmel Sketchbook, Book VI, page 1; DMMC, WM, 59x5.6.*

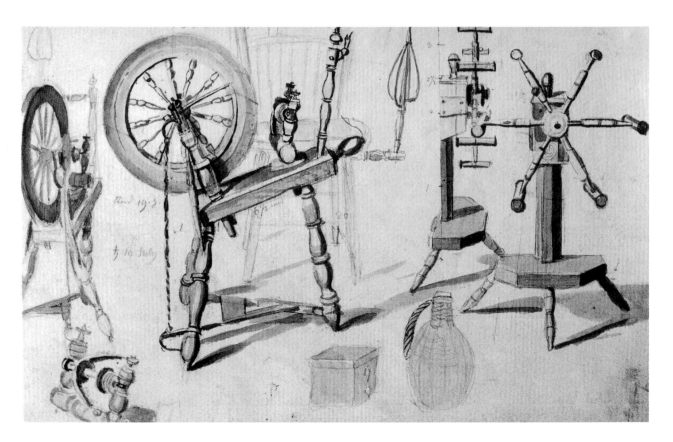

Figure 4 (left). Detail of a Boston fishing-lady-type needlework picture, showing the method of using a hand-held drop spindle. Polychrome canvas work in tent stitch, with crewel yarns. Boston, 1745–1755.

Figure 5 (right). Spinning wheel, niddy-noddy, and hetchel with combed flax. United States, 1780–1840. *Niddy-noddy from author's collection.*

To measure and wrap the finished yarns into skeins or hanks, a niddy-noddy or clock reel (figure 5) was used, although this activity was also done by hand. Much of the home-produced yarn was then sent out to professional weavers, most of whom were men, to be woven into cloth. Some weavers also fulled and dyed the completed cloth or the fulling and dyeing might be done by a separate concern. In either case, the cloth was then returned to the housewife, who cut it according to her needs for household linens or the family's wardrobe.

Because it took so much effort and expense to create even one piece of cloth, the basic wardrobe was simple and sparse. For a common woman, it might consist of a long shift or two (which also served as underwear and nightgown), a number of petticoats, a waistcoat, an apron, one or two caps, stockings, and a pair of shoes. Layers of petticoats were added or shed as the temperature and fashion dictated. The clothing of men of average means

Figure 6. Illustrations like this one from London's *Ladies Magazine* were the primary way fashions passed from England to the colonies. Here is the latest design for August 1770 showing "A Lady in Full Dress." Notice the long, cone-shaped bodice, heavily trimmed with lace. Photograph by L. Delmar Swan. *Author's collection.*

was similarly basic: a shorter shift (the top part of which often had a collar and served as a shirt on warm days), simple britches often of leather, a few shirts, a jacket, a hat, shoes, and stockings.

Worn garments usually served as patterns when constructing new clothing. Only fashion-conscious women consulted the engravings published in European magazines, such as the *Ladies Magazine* from London, or sought sketches and directions from relatives and friends (figure 6). For instance, in a letter written to her mother in 1797, Eliza Southgate, a Maine girl born in 1783, asked for patterns for gowns to be sent so that she could choose one to make a gown for herself.[1]

Sometimes a woman would make clothing for a fashion doll, also called a "baby." Some of these were commercially produced in England and France. The doll clothing illustrated in miniature a favorite dress or new fashion, and a woman would send it to a female friend or relative to use as inspiration for work on her own wardrobe. For example, in 1781 Rebecca Franks, a woman of means from Philadelphia, wrote her sister Abigail in Flatbush, "Nanny Van Horn and self were employed yesterday morning in trying to dress a rag baby in the fashion, but could not succeed. It shall however go, as 'twill in some degree give you an idea of the fashion as to the Jacket and pinning on the handkerchief."[2]

These miniature fashions were also created by dressmakers, or mantua-makers as they were known, as a way to illustrate their designs to their patrons. In 1756, mantua-makers Mary Wallace and Clementine Ferguson advertised in the *New York Mercury* that they had "fashions in miniature" for both ladies and gentlemen.

After the customer had selected a design from the miniature forms displayed, the mantua-maker would cut the expensive silk and/or woolen fabrics chosen and fit the pieces directly on the customer. The final tasks were to stitch, line, and trim—often in a complicated manner—the garment.

Sometimes a mantua-maker or a skillful amateur seamstress would come into the home of a woman to cut out a dress. Then the woman would assist her by stitching the seams and hems. In her diary, Elizabeth Sandwith Drinker, member of a prominent Philadelphia Quaker family, mentioned that "Betsy Fordham sewing for us for the present. I have been busy with her for near three weeks, and am almost tir'd of confindment." Betsy Fordham was undoubtedly a professional seamstress who cut and fitted garments and did the fine work on them, leaving Mrs. Drinker to sew the seams. According to the Drinker diary, as the women worked, Molly Drinker, a daughter, read a novel to the older women, although novel reading by females was much criticized. Mrs. Drinker noted in defense, "'tis seldom I listen to a romance, nor would I encourage my Children doing much of that business." Apparently, the tedium of this plain sewing warranted an exception.[3]

Born into a prosperous Philadelphia Quaker family in 1735, Elizabeth Sandwith married Henry Drinker, a widower and successful prominent Quaker, in 1761. They had nine children, but only five survived. For fifty years she recorded many intimate thoughts and attitudes of the day, keeping a diary until just before her death in 1807. Because this diary spans such a long time period and because it is the most informative diary kept by any early American woman, I will repeatedly refer to it in this text.

Young girls contributed to a family's plain sewing by knitting (see

Figure 7. Three pairs of knitted stockings, one with the initials I L knitted in. United States, 1800–1840.

Glossary). Almost all girls—and some boys—learned to knit by the age of six. Stockings and mittens were always needed, and young hands could manage these simple but important contributions to the household well. The every day stockings they fashioned often bore numbers or initials to facilitate matching them into pairs, which in a large family might otherwise be time-consuming. Sometimes this mark was knit right into the stocking, or it might be embroidered on in a contrasting color (figure 7). For many children, marking was their first attempt at embroidery.

Like other kinds of plain sewing, knitting could be a pleasant task.

Once learned, it was so simple and mechanical that it did not inhibit conversation. Moreover, because it required little light, it was an ideal evening activity. In her diary, Sarah Anna Emery recalled with obvious nostalgia the fall evenings of her girlhood in Newbury, Massachusetts, when "the winter's stocking yarn was . . . carded and spun, and the lengthening evenings . . . [were] enlivened by the busy click of knitting needles."[4]

As she did her part of the plain sewing under the watchful guidance of an older female, usually her mother, a young girl began to understand the expectations that society held for a woman. Listening as she worked to her elders gossip or exchange news, she could absorb the attitudes and role expectations that would shape her later life. Here she would begin to grasp the implicit assumption that a woman must marry, even if no one told her so explicitly. As a result, most girls aspired to marry well and have a household to run for a husband.

In preparation for housewifery and motherhood, plain sewing was only the start of the skills an eighteenth-century girl needed to know. To later be considered competent, it was crucial for her to be well trained in all the skills of housewifery. This training, which was sometimes her only education, was usually acquired at home, from her mother, but some girls were trained in the household of a relative or as indentured servants. In return for food, clothing, and lodging, these girls, often as young as age eight, learned how to serve their new households in the various roles they would later assume as housewives: cooks, housekeepers, washing women, seamstresses, and nursemaids.

The practice of indenturing relieved a girl's family of the cost of supporting her, and it provided a more prosperous family with a relatively cheap servant. The arrangement was formalized in an indenture contract, which specified the parties, the term of service (for girls the average term agreed on ranged between seven to ten years), and the obligations of both the master and the young servant, including the freedom dues that the master was to pay the servant when her term expired.

Very few girls were apprenticed to skilled professionals, such as mantua-makers, embroiderers, upholsterers, bakers, corset makers, or milliners. Young males, however, were almost always apprenticed to specific tradesmen after they had reached the age of fourteen or so. By far the greatest percentage of girls who were sent away from home learned housewifery.

The roles of these young housewifery apprentices varied considerably from family to family. Late in the eighteenth century, a Frenchman observed that in New England, where extremes in wealth were less apparent than elsewhere in the land, indentured servants were frequently the children of a neighbor or a relative. They were considered more or less equal in station to the children of the house and were treated accordingly, being allowed, for instance, to eat at the same table with the master's family.[5] In other circumstances, the typical indentured servant was more servile. Sarah Emery remembered,

> *In most families there was a boy or girl bound to service until the age of eighteen. When the hour [tea time] arrived this young servant passed round napkins upon a salver; next a man or maid servant bore round the tray of cups, the young waiter following with cream and sugar. Bread and butter and cake succeeded only, these were passed round two or three times and the young servant stood, salver in hand ready to take the cups to be replenished.[6]*

Not all masters treated their servants kindly. Sarah Emery also recalled a minister who bound and whipped his servant girl for slight offenses and, on occasion, contrived to tie her tongue to her great toe.[7] Unlike their male counterparts, female servants seldom believed in the efficacy of running away from an abusive or demanding master.

For any girl, indentured or not, marrying well was the best route to improving her social position. For an indentured girl, the chances of making a good match increased if she worked in a more affluent home where she could meet the prosperous artisans who did business with the family she served. To sweeten a daughter's allure to prospective suitors, many fathers tried to win a provision in the indenture contract for freedom dues that would serve the girl as a dowry.

One typical young girl, Sarah Wade, was indentured in 1827 (figure 8) to a merchant and his wife in Lancaster County, Pennsylvania, to "learn the art, trade, and mystery [of] Housewifery" and to receive nine months' schooling. The settlement that her indenture contract called for upon

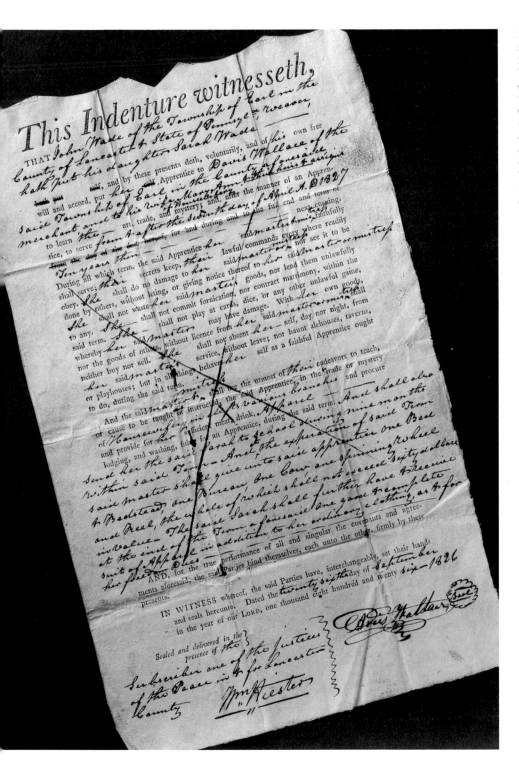

Figure 8. A printed indenture form filled in on September 26, 1826. The father of Sarah Wade indentured her to merchant David Wallace and his wife, Mary Ann, of Lancaster County, Pennsylvania, starting the following year. Legal documents deliberately had a distinctive cut between the copies given the two parties. The large "X" running through the words proves that Sarah completed her term. *DMMC, WM, 76x98.117.*

completion of her ten-year term was a rather generous one: "one Bed & Bedstead, one Bureau, one Cow, one spinning Wheel and Reel, the whole of which shall not exceed sixty dollars." She was also to be awarded "one good and complete suit of Apparel," a provision that was standard for later indenture contracts.[8]

By the time an indentured girl had served out her time, she was presumed to be emotionally as well as technically prepared for taking on the duties of adulthood. Similarly, her teenage counterparts who had not been indentured were considered ready to assume the obligations of a woman—marriage, household management, childbirth, and rearing children—all of which required both physical and personal strength.

A PREGNANT WOMAN would carry on normal social and work activities in addition to preparing the clothing and bedding that she would need for the baby (figures 9, 10, and 11). When the expectant mother went into labor, a midwife would come to the house and stay until shortly after the birth of the baby. Despite the proficiency of the midwives, and later in the eighteenth century male physicians, any complications during birth could cause serious problems.

Adding to the difficulty of childbirth was the lack of anesthetics. Women were often denied the few painkillers, such as liquor, that were in use. In Genesis God had promised Eve that "in sorrow thou shalt bring forth children." To the more literal colonists, this was justification enough for denying women the minimal relief available to them (figure 12). Cotton Mather, the famous Puritan minister of Boston whose career spanned the late seventeenth and early eighteenth centuries, believed that women in childbirth should have the same consciousness as anyone else in danger of dying. He wrote that a dutiful woman must prepare in happiness for birth, realizing and repenting her sins because she might sacrifice her life on the day of birth.[9]

An expectant mother could draw comfort from the fact that, if it came to a choice, a midwife would attempt to save her life at the expense of

Figure 9. Baby cap with needle lace lace insert worked in white linen with fine white linen thread. It also has tiny spaced sprigs, done in satin and whip stitches. Probably made by Deborah Hunt Jefferies of Wilmington, Delaware, for the birth of her daughter Ann in 1791. H. 5 3/4"; W. 4 1/4".

a child's, rather than vice versa. Not until about 1780 did male physicians practice regularly in this country, and their attendance at childbirth was unusual until the early nineteenth century. In *Outlines of the Theory and*

Figure 10 (left). Unusual swinging cradle made of pine and maple, supported on a trestle base. Child experts such as Dr. Buchan considered the swinging motion preferable to the more vigorous rocking of a regular cradle. Interior painted mustard yellow, exterior blue green. One-piece quilt of French printed cotton, worked in running stitches in a pattern of scallops and diamonds. United States, 1800–1830.

Figure 11 (opposite). One-piece white crib quilt worked in running stitch with accents of cross stitch; wooden doll in white muslin dress embroidered with cotton satin and eyelet stitches around the neck. Pennsylvania walnut cradle with knobs on the side for lacing in an active baby. Rug is embroidered and shirred. United States, 1775–1825.

Practice of Midwifery, published in 1775, English physician Dr. Alexander Hamilton stated that the doctor had a duty to give "perfect safety to the mother, who is always justly entitled to the first place in our intentions."[10]

If a mother survived the ordeal of childbirth, there was no assurance that her child would. The survival rates for children were grim. One in ten did not survive the first year, and almost four in ten died before age six. Diseases such as measles, diphtheria, whooping cough, mumps, and chicken pox often proved fatal. Eighteenth- and early nineteenth-century cities and towns were repeatedly visited by dysentery, smallpox, and, particularly in Philadelphia, yellow fever, to all of which the very young and the elderly were especially susceptible.

If a child survived these illnesses and some of the equally dangerous cures such as bleeding, other hazards and mishaps awaited. Elizabeth Drinker's diary records many instances: "A little girl of 6 years lost her life

in a necessary [privy] into which she had fell . . . two little children in ye
Jersyes [New Jersey] some days ago, wandered out of their knowledge in the
woods, and were not found 'till the third day . . . one is likely to recover, the
other not." Two parents had "lost a little Daugh'r . . . between 2 and 3 years
of age, she was left alone last night for a short time, and fell into the fier . . .
she expired before morn'g."[11]

Letters and diaries written by individuals of all classes in both urban

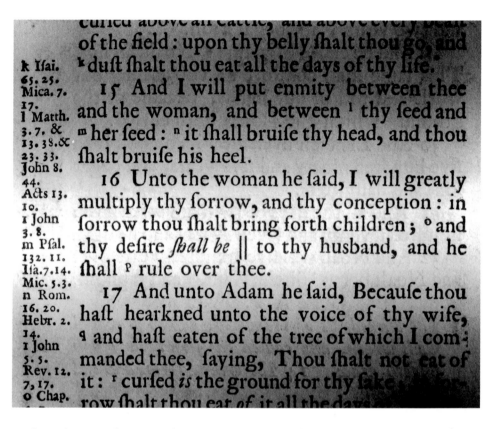

Figure 12. Genesis 3:16, sometimes referred to as "The Curse of Eve." This Bible was printed in Dublin, Ireland, in 1741.

and rural areas often reveal a preoccupation with illnesses and a sense of helplessness in coping with them. Tuberculosis in particular, referred to as "spitting blood" or "galloping consumption," is mentioned with dread in many diaries.

Although they took less of a toll in America than in Europe, with its crowded and unfavorable sanitary conditions, epidemics were common and the measures taken to combat them ineffectual. An enfeebled Abigail Adams informed her husband on September 8, 1775, that violent dysentery had already killed his brother Isaac and was sweeping through her household. Abigail had it herself when she wrote, "Our little Tommy was next, and he lies very ill now . . . Yesterday Patty was seized . . . Our house is a hospital in every part; and what with my own weakness and distress of mind for my family, I have been unhappy enough."[12]

Figure 13. Signs of illness or death: a doctor's chest; a bleeder (the small J-shaped tool in the foreground); a silver pap boat, on the left; an early silver spout cup, on the right, for feeding invalids.

With death constantly so close at hand, everyone including children learned to function while being continually aware of their own mortality (figure 13). When Cotton Mather addressed himself to sick children, he reminded them to repent their sins lest they die soon. Unlike later revival ministers, Mather sought not to frighten them but only to urge them to prepare for the uncertain moment when they would face God's judgment.[13] Unfortunately, this approach probably produced more dread of death than resolution in facing up to it, since it was devilishly difficult to know whether or when one was spiritually pure enough to meet one's Maker. The threat of death could not be mitigated; it just had to be accepted. And it was never too early to teach a child to start.

In this arduous life, children who were disciplined, obedient, and unspoiled were not only best prepared for coping with the rigors of life and the imminence of death but were also best able to assist the family and the community. William Kenrick, English author of *The Whole Duty of a Woman,* warned mothers against showering their offspring with "an excess of thy love." He advised a mother to distance herself from her children both as a means of lessening her grief if they should die and as a way of preventing children from becoming spoiled, indulged creatures who would "bring a curse upon thee and not a blessing."[14]

Perhaps the most dramatic indication of parents' thoroughly practical view of their children was the way they dressed them, which for those of average means was unpretentiously. As young children, both boys and girls wore smocks or gowns, a fashion that continued almost to the twentieth century in many families. At about age six, boys were put into either pants or breeches like their fathers', and girls continued to wear smocks or dresses. Before this changeover, which was distinct for boys but barely noticeable for girls, affluent families took to dressing their young boys and girls on special occasions in the elaborate attire of fancy ladies (figure 14). At these times, such as for portrait sittings, the children resembled mock adults, as if to emphasize their innocence and protected status. None of this had an effect on poorer children, who were likely to be dressed in whatever clothes were available and were treated as adults as soon as possible.

English physician Dr. William Buchan advocated allowing boys to enjoy the loose gowns of childhood beyond the age of six. he complained, "Silly mothers are very impatient to strip them [boys] of their loose frocks and make them look like little men."[15] Obviously, this "breeching" was an important event for a boy. The radical change from a skirt to breeches visibly marked the beginning of his new adult role. But for a girl, the change from infant's to adult's clothing hardly mattered, since the difference was so slight.

Figure 14. Portrait of a young boy, probably Benjamin Badger, painted by his father, Joseph Badger. He wears a blue dress with an orange red petticoat and holds his pet squirrel. Boston; 1758–60.

THE REARING OF children added enormously to a woman's responsibilities. Although husbands usually exercised final authority in matters of discipline, mothers had the routine responsibility for looking after the children. They often found it a difficult responsibility to cope with. Esther Burr reflected after the birth of her second child, the famous Aaron Burr, in 1756, "When I had but one child my hands were tied, but now I am tied hand and foot [with two]; how I shall get along when I have got 1/2 dzn or 10 children I cant devise."[15]

In addition to bringing up the children, Mrs. Burr and all other mothers had a seemingly endless stream of household chores to do, many of which could not await the return of the husband from his shop or the fields. Routinely, a woman tended the vegetable garden, drew water, maintained the fire, cooked, preserved food, and cleaned. All these chores were in addition to sewing, which entailed a whole separate range of tasks. Assistance sometimes came from other women: paid help, slaves, indentured servants, daughters, the family spinster, or other relatives. But few women were able to escape the household drudgery. Even women who had servants or family help were responsible for overseeing the satisfactory completion of the work.

Few records illuminate the routine of daily chores. Most were so repetitive and boring that they warranted little space in letters and diaries. In any case, these were usually written by the more affluent, better-educated women, who had servants to perform most of the menial chores.

Cooking was probably the single most time-consuming of the daily tasks. Basic cooking was held in such low regard that it was taught only in the home (figure 15). If one learned cooking outside the home, it was of a fancier sort, such as pastry making. Women avoided as much of the basic cooking as they could, using children, servants, and even dogs to relieve them. Spit-dogs were a special breed of "little bow-legged dogs" trained to rotate the spit over the fire by running beside it in a hollow cylinder. One observer tells us, "As cooking time approached, it was no uncommon thing to see the cooks running about the street looking up their truant [dog] labourers" (figure 16)[16] Some families purchased an elaborate clock jack to

Figure 15. Writing on the rim of this earthenware plate, the potter Samuel Troxel ascribed the following culinary credo to his wife: "I only cook what I can cook still; what the pig won't eat my husband will." Upper Hanover Township, Pennsylvania; dated January 20, 1846.

turn the spit. This device worked with weights, much like a conventional clock. At least by the end of the eighteenth century, city women could buy prepared foods. Architectural evidence indicates that very few interior or exterior ovens have been found in old Philadelphia houses, a signal that women were cooking less.

Although clothes (like people) were washed infrequently, their up-keep did require some attention. For laces, silks, and other elaborate fabrics, there were professional cleaners, but the washing of everyday linens and cottons was usually a household chore. Elizabeth Drinker, married for thirty-three years, wrote, "we hir'd a dutch woman nam'd Rosanna to

The pye from Bake-house she had brought / & let it fall for want of thought | The ACCIDENT in LOMBARD-STREET PHILAD.ᵃ 1787 *designed & engraved by C.W. Peale* | And laughing Sweeps collect around / The pye that's scatter'd on the ground   N.ᵒ 1

Figure 16. Not all city women did their own baking. *The Accident in Lombard-Street* shows a servant who is upset at having just dropped the pie she was carrying from the bakery. The chimney sweeps and even the dogs gather around to laugh at her. To the left, another woman carries home her pie. Etching by Charles Willson Peale, dated November, 1787.

NOTES

1. Bowne, *Girl's Life*, 10.
2. Franks, "Letter of Miss Rebecca Franks," 307.
3. Diary of Elizabeth Drinker, June 20, 1795. The author read all of the original manuscript and typescript copies of Elizabeth Sandwith Drinker's diary held in the Historical Society of Pennsylvania in the 1970s. Since then a fine three-volume, carefully annotated, diary, *The Diary of Elizabeth Drinker*, has been edited by Elaine Forman Crane (Boston, Northeastern University Press, 1991).
4. Emery, *Reminiscences*, 8.
5. *Observations sur les Moeurs*.
6. Emery, *Reminiscences*, 245, 200.
7. Emery, *Reminiscences*, 200.
8. Indenture of Sarah Wade.
9. Mather, *Elizabeth in her Holy Retirement*, 6–7.
10. Hamilton, *Outlines*, 214.
11. Diary of Elizabeth Drinker, July 1, 1781; December 5, 1794.
12. Adams, *Familiar Letters*, 95.
13. Mather, *Diary*, vol. 2, 104.
14. [Kenrick], *Whole Duty*, vol. 1, 50.
15. Journal of Esther Burr, April 13, 1756.
16. Watson, *Annals*, 350.
17. Diary of Elizabeth Drinker, June 7, 1794.
18. Wister, *Sally Wister's Journal*, 182.
19. Pennington, "Unfortunate Mother's Advice," 146.
20. "Letter from a Brother to a Sister," 260.
21. [Farfar], *Friend*, 122.
22. [Farfar], *Friend*, 14.

2. Molding the Accomplished Miss

Figure 17 (opposite). Susan Smith embroidered her solidly-worked sampler of the First Baptist Meeting House of Providence, Rhode Island, while attending the Balch School there. The date at the top, October 29, 1793, and the "wrought" date of May 9, 1794, may be the dates she started and finished this work. Susan used both embroidery and canvas work stitches: whip, satin, seed, Queen's, double cross, tent, and cross. The silk threads are predominantly dark and light green with accents of brown, tan, white, and blue. H. and W. 16 3/4".

Matrimony. Wanted, by a young gentleman just beginning housekeeping, a Lady, between 18 and 20 years of age, with a good education, and a fortune not less than 5000 £s, 5 feet 4 inches without her shoes, not fat nor lean, a clear skin, a sweet breath, with a good set of teeth, no pride or affectation; not very talkative, nor one that is dumb; no scold, but of a spirit to relent an affront; of a charitable disposition; not over fond of dress, through always decent and clean; that will entertain her husband's friends with affability and cheerfulness, and prefer his company to publick diversions and gadding about; one who will keep his secrets, that he may open his heart to her at all times without reserve; that can extend domestick expences with economy, as prosperity advances, without ostentation, and retrench them with cheerfulness, should the occasion require.

Any lady answering this description, and disposed for matrimony, is desired to direct to O.C. to be left at the Post Office in Savannah.

N. B. None need apply who fail in any one particular.

—advertisement in the *Gazette of the State of Georgia*, published in Savannah on July 1, 1784

THIS ADVERTISER'S IDEA of the model bride closely resembled the ideal that well-off young ladies of the period aspired to in order to please a man. The would-be husband planned to be the center of his wife's world. He expected his wife to be not only competent but loyal, discreet, cheerful, and above all devoted—a tall order, to say the least. No wonder many a girl spent her entire youth and adolescence being cultivated to be a wife.

Even before a girl could grasp the notion that a woman needed to be married, her upbringing was working to ensure that she would be. From at least the age of five until she married, her education consisted primarily of schooling in the traits that would make her appealing to a prospective husband, and a good wife and mother. These traits included not only the practical skills of housewifery but, as our advertiser above was careful to detail, the attitudes characteristic of a proper woman.

As she prepared for marriage and adulthood, a girl received an education whose quality depended on how close she lived to a school, the wealth of her parents, and perhaps most of all her parents' attitudes toward the education of females. If the parents' aspirations for their daughter were limited to finding her an acceptable match, her education was likely to be poor. And this appeared to be the norm. Historians such as Kenneth A. Lockridge attempted to decipher the literacy rate by studying the signatures on deeds in colonial New England. Lockridge found that these signatures were the best present-day confirmation of the ability to read and write. By 1790, literacy among males in New England led the country at a rate close to eighty-five percent. While the women's literacy rate was below twenty percent in the seventeenth century, it improved to about fifty percent by the mid-nineteenth century. Others have estimated that by the beginning of the nineteenth century, about half the female population in America was not literate, although most white men were at least functionally literate. For example, Elizabeth Drinker, hardly a woman without means, remarked with dismay in 1799 that her nine-year-old granddaughter could not yet read.[1]

As a rule, education for girls ranked behind that for boys, the education of the latter being itself unimpressive. Even in New England, whose Puritan population professed a strong interest in education if only to enable one to read the Bible, it was not uncommon for a girl to be able to read but still be unable to write her name. Reading and writing were considered as separate skills at this time. Few areas offered free education to either boys or girls; the payment could be in money or in such things as sharing the boarding of the teacher or supplying wood. In the first half of the seventeenth century, the Colony of Massachusetts required towns of more than fifty families to establish a grammar school, yet few were actually created before the eighteenth century. Most communities found it cheaper to pay the fine each year for breaking the law than to build a school and hire a teacher.

In the South, fathers who could afford it might join with their neighbors to hire a tutor to teach their children. Girls were usually allowed to participate in these classes as long as their interests or abilities warranted. In rare cases, a well-read father would permit a particularly promising girl to be tutored with the boys who were preparing for college. Or an exceptional father might teach his daughter advanced subjects himself.

It was not until 1825 that the first free public high schools for women opened, in New York city and Boston. By 1870, there were only 160 high schools, primarily coeducational, in the whole country.

Boys training for a career such as commerce usually attended "English schools," which stressed reading, grammar, mathematics, science, and geography. Boys studying law or for the ministry went to a similar institution, the grammar or classical school, which added Greek and Latin to the curriculum. Sarah Emery, of Newbury, Massachusetts, recorded that a girl in her area could attend the grammar school for an hour and a half per day in the summer—after the boys' session had ended—if the girl's parents paid taxes of at least three hundred pounds per year. Some years later the girls attended the schools from six to eight o'clock in the morning, before the boys' classes.[2] With such arrangements, a girl could not help but realize that even among the prosperous, the education of a girl was at best of secondary concern.

Among the very few who expressed exception to this indifference to the education of girls was Quaker Anthony Benezet, a mid-eighteenth-century Philadelphian who had perhaps the greatest impact. Periodically from 1754 to 1777, he taught daughters of the best Philadelphia families reading, writing, arithmetic, and English grammar. He also advocated education for black children and, for a short time, ran a morning school for girls.

BEFORE THE AGE at which she might, if she were lucky, attend a grammar school, a young girl might be sent to the early American equivalent of nursery school: the dame school. For many girls this provided all the formal schooling they would receive during their lifetimes. Far from a formal setting, it consisted of a small neighborhood class taught by one woman, the dame, in her home. The pupils, both boys and girls, attended haphazardly and for widely varying periods. Some children began as early as age three, others as late as age ten.

The teacher made some attempt to teach reading and, perhaps, some "figuring," but for the girls at least, the most common activity was practicing the plain sewing stitches and knitting that they were likely to have begun learning at home from their mothers at about this age (figure 18). These schools, which survived from the seventeenth century until well into the nineteenth, were essentially private schools, because the teachers were compensated in some manner by the students' parents.

Dame school was not necessarily a pleasant learning experience. Until nearly 1800, children were considered to be marked by original sin; hence this first training was aimed at taming their will and stamping out pride and stubbornness. This attitude toward children had softened a bit by 1830, when a book entitled *The Token* published a nostalgic representation of a dame school (figure 19). Accompanying the picture was a poem:

> *The hour-glass in its guarded nook,*
> *Which oft our tiny fingers shook*
> *By stealth, if flowed to slow away*
> *The sand that held us from our play.*[3]

The artist and poet here evidently worried little about original sin in these children. If anything, the children look almost angelic, though one notes a hint of mischief in the eyes of those not immediately under the gaze of the schoolmistress. She, drooping and bored, seems to have been a typical dame.

After dame school, a girl might move on to a sewing class, again a small group taught by one woman in her home, but not likely to be in the immediate neighborhood unless the girl lived in a big city or fair-sized town. The out-of-town girls usually stayed with relatives or friends of the family, but some boarded with the teacher's own family. This arrangement was more convenient for the student and more lucrative for the teacher. Attending such a school allowed a girl from the country not only to learn fancy needlework, her most important accomplishment, but to widen her acquaintances among a new group of eligible young men.

We know from a 1687 letter written by Boston businessman and judge Samuel Sewall to his cousin in England that such schools existed even in seventeenth-century America. Sewall reported that his daughters were about to attend school and asked his cousin to send a large supply of fustian and crewels (see Glossary) for bed hangings and chair coverings to keep them "out of Idleness."[4] Undoubtedly, this school was a private sewing class for young ladies, taught by the local expert. Apparently, his daughters already knew plain sewing and some embroidery, and they were now prepared to do a large, expensive project under a teacher's supervision.

Schools that taught only needlework were common in all towns and cities in colonial America. More ambitious schools, usually run by sisters or spouses, offered instruction in other accomplishments, such as drawing, dancing, and occasionally English or French. After 1750, successful sewing schools expanded, arranging for visits from teachers of music, English, and French. These institutions were the forerunners of the true boarding school, or young ladies' school, common late in the century and through the mid-nineteenth century, which offered not only accomplishments but some scholastic subjects. Boarding schools were more likely to provide room and board for their pupils, though town girls who attended them lived at home.

The early, one-subject classes were loosely structured, more like dame schools for older girls than formal educational institutions. The teachers advertised as private tutorial services—"at the house of Sarah Haigh," for example—and not by a formal name. The pupils could be as young as eight or as old as sixteen. They stayed for anywhere from one to three years, attending class with varying degrees of regularity.

Twelve-year-old Anna Green Winslow, who went in 1771 from Nova Scotia to live with her aunt in Boston, seems to have been a typical student, both in patronizing different schools for different subjects and in her erratic attendance. She went to Mrs. Smith's needlework school several afternoons a week, a dancing class run by a Mr. Turner—where she wore "black feathers on [her] head"—and a writing school.[5] Her diary discloses that she frequently skipped classes, dissuaded by bad weather, feelings of ennui, or just the possibility of a more promising activity elsewhere.

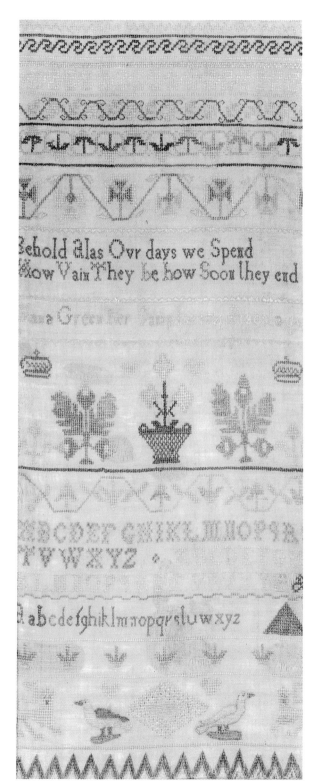

Figure 20. Anna Green's 1741 long, narrow sampler, while out of fashion for the time, shows a strong English influence with its pair of crowns and lions. She included the name Piscataqua, which apparently was used then as a general term for the river and the towns along it. The stitches include cross, tent, eyelet, Irish, satin, and Queen's. Anna Green was the mother of Anna Green Winslow, who wrote a brief, colorful diary of her Boston school days (see Bibliography). H. 20 1/4"; W. 8 1/8".

IN NEEDLEWORK CLASSES and even earlier, in dame schools, almost every girl worked a sampler (see Glossary), a piece in which she would demonstrate her needlework prowess (figure 20). The sampler is one of the most intriguing forms of early American needlework we have. Certainly it was a long-popular art form, practiced by the earliest immigrants and still produced well into the nineteenth century. It virtually chronicled needlework styles as they were changing, since the fashionable fancywork of any particular day invariably found its way into samplers. Moreover, the sampler itself gradually changed form. The vague definition in Webster's 1806 *Compendious Dictionary*, "a piece of a girl's needlework, a pattern," hints that the sampler was anything but a set form.

The whereabouts of at least seven seventeenth-century colonial samplers are currently known. All were made in Massachusetts Colony, and three are now owned by Winterthur Museum (figures 21, 22, and 23). They are long and narrow, without design borders. The patterns found on them were in the repertoire of designs used in English samplers by 1630. These designs, in turn, had their antecedents in patterns developed in the Middle East and Italy.[6]

Loara Standish made the earliest known American sampler, probably completed about 1640. She was the daughter of Barbara and Miles Standish and lived in Duxbury, Massachusetts. This piece is typical of seventeenth-century samplers made in England and America in that it is narrow and long (seven by twenty-three inches). The length of the sampler is actually a loom width; the shorter top and bottom edges are the two selvage edges. It displays a variety of horizontal bands and a verse.

Figure 21 (opposite left). Thirteen-year-old Sarah Collins of Salem, Massachusetts, worked this 1673 sampler. The top alphabet, worked in cross stitch, is erratic; upper and lower case letters are mixed and some letters in common use at that time. are missing. The second alphabet is in eyelet stitch, the third in satin. The wide light-colored band pattern, third from the top, is the same as the band second from the top on Sarah Stone's sampler. Both are worked in double running stitch. H. 17 1/2"; W. 8 1/2".

Figure 22 (opposite right). Sarah Stone, also from Salem, worked a verse instead of an alphabet, in satin and eyelet stitches: "That God is Mine / AS SureLY I kNOW / Because MY BLeSS / ed Iesus Made him / so Sarah Stone / 1678." Other stitches include cross, eyelet, double running, and satin with some padding underneath. The colors are blue, greens, beiges, and browns. H. 16 3/4"; W. 7 5/8".

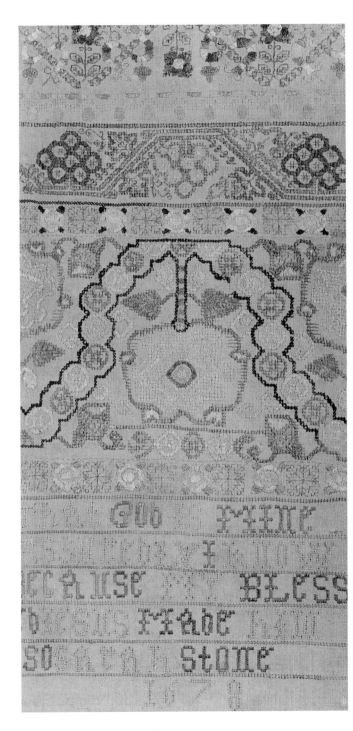

Figure 23. The upper third of Mehitable Payson's sampler is worked in blues, light green, and medium and light brown silk; the lower portion is done entirely in white linen thread. Made between 1698 and 1706 in Rawley, Massachusetts, this is currently the earliest known American example of needle lace. The upper portion is worked in various reversible stitches including double running. The white work section below it features satin stitch, drawn work, cutwork, and detached buttonhole. H. 24"; W. 5 1/2".

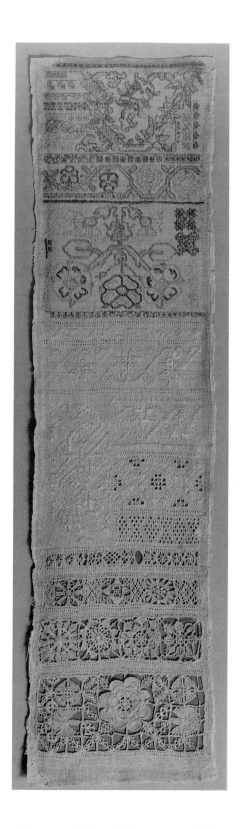

One band used in Sarah Collins's 1673 sampler (figure 21) also appears in Sarah Stone's 1678 work (figure 22). Numerous other bands are common to two or more of the early American samplers. The complexity of many of the designs and stitches suggests that they were passed from teacher or parent to student.

The 1694 will of Elizabeth Brunson of Farmington, Connecticut, provided that her "white worked Sampler" be given to her granddaughter Elizabeth.[7] A unique survivor among the seven Massachusetts samplers is Mehitable Payson's work, which includes bands of white work and cutwork lace (see Glossary) worked in linen thread on linen (figure 23) Probably made between 1698 and 1706, Mehitable's needle lace bands reflect the contemporary fashion for this kind of lace on clothing. The colonial regulations governing who was allowed to wear or own lace became increasingly difficult to enforce by the end of the seventeenth century.

During the eighteenth century, the long narrow form of samplers gradually shortened and widened. Those made in New England tended to change more slowly than samplers made in the Philadelphia area. By 1725, Philadelphia samplers had become wider and shorter, and they soon displayed decorative borders all around (figure 24).[8]

During the eighteenth century, sampler shapes became even wider rectangles, and occasionally were square (plate 4). Early in the nineteenth century some samplers became wider than high. Girls almost always signed their samplers and embroidered their birthday or the date they finished the work.

In the eighteenth century most girls from well-to-do families worked two samplers: a simple marking sampler (figure 18), often done in dame school, and later a more decorative, fancy sampler. On the marking sampler a girl worked an alphabet (this exercise may have been her first encounter with letters) in cross stitch (see Glossary) as preparation for the marking of initials on linens and clothing (figure 2). It was necessary to stitch initials on fabric items rather than to use a pen because before 1830 inks rotted the fabric. Then came the fancy sampler and/or a needlework picture, two forms that by the mid-eighteenth century often closely resembled one another (plate 5 and figure 27). Needlework pictures sometimes carried names

and dates, just like samplers. Only the lack of alphabets and verses differentiated them from samplers.

The makers of these samplers and pictures prized their works as emblems of the accomplished ladies they were becoming. Many samplers and needlework pictures made between 1785 and 1810 were such intricate projects that even an industrious girl needed months to complete one (figures 25 and 26). Obviously, such a major project was a source of great family pride when it was finished. Parents selected particularly fine ones to be hung up for display, and the girls who made these pieces reveled in the praise they elicited. Sarah Emery recalled, "I became perfectly entranced over . . . [my] sampler that was much admired."[9]

Sally Wister noted that a Southern officer who was visiting Philadelphia during the Revolutionary War, "observ'd my sampler, which was in full view. [He] wished I would teach the Virginians some of my needle wisdom; they were the laziest girls in the world." This sampler, still in existence, was done at Ann Marsh's school. It is similar to, but smaller and less elaborate than, an earlier piece worked by Elizabeth Rush and shown in figure 24.[10]

As a woman grew older, her sampler or needlework picture became one of her most cherished possessions. She might bequeath it in her will, as Elizabeth Brunson did with her sampler, or present it to a favorite young female relative as a gift, as Sarah Wistar did with her needlework picture (plate 6). In 1834, years after she had made her sampler, Mrs. Caroline Gilman remembered it with pride in *Recollections of a Housekeeper*. She wrote,

Figure 24 (opposite). Shorter and wider framed samplers appeared in Philadelphia as early as 1725. Eleven years later this style, similar but slightly more elaborate, appeared. The sampler is marked "1734 EliZabeth RUsh her WOrk done in the th year of her AGe." (Elizabeth purposely omitted her age.) She also included the typical phrase: "This work in [hand] my friends may have/when i am dead and laid in my grave." Silk yarns in bright blues, yellows, greens, reds, and pink on a fine linen ground, intricately worked in cross, Queen's, satin, and whip stitches. This general sampler style remained popular for another sixty years in the Philadelphia area, though later renditions of it were worked less skillfully. Elizabeth was probably the great-aunt of Dr. Benjamin Rush, a signer of the Declaration of Independence and an outspoken advocate of better education for women. H. 18 1/4"; W. 13".

Figure 25 (right). A group of Boston samplers is currently identified because of their narrow upper bands and a distinctive lower band of hexagons. Many of these samplers also feature an Adam and Eve panel. This, by Hepzebah Baker, dated 1738, portrays a tree, birds, and vases in the lower panel. H. 18 1/4"; W. 8 1/2".

Figure 26 (opposite). Lydia Fitch used stylish alphabets for her day. Probably intended to be a solidly worked sampler, she gave up after trying to fill in with black cross stitches around the letters. The lower panel started out well with graceful trees and small flowers, but the urn was overwhelmed by a pink flower. Her name, age, Suffield (Connecticut), and date, 1793, are worked in eyelet stitches. The urn handles and finer lines are tightly pulled buttonhole stitches. H. 11"; W. 11".

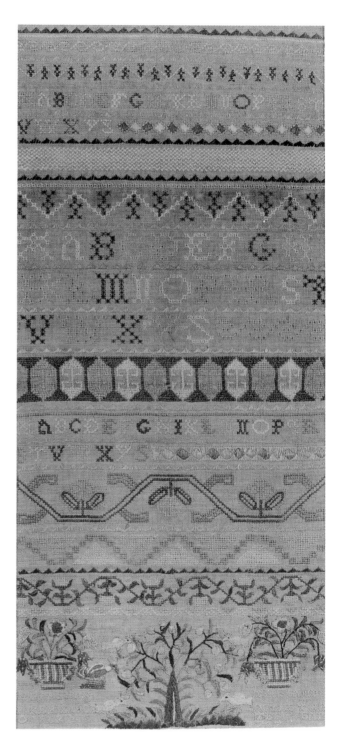

A B C D E F G H I J K L M N O P Q
R S T U V W X Y Z & abcdefgh
ijklmnopqrstuvwxyz&
A B C D E F G H I J K L M N O
P Q R S T U V W X Y Z & 12
345678910 LYDIA FITCH of
Suffield Aged Ten Years
March Eighteenth 1790

Figure 27 (right). While the original design for this embroidery came from seventeenth-century France, Priscilla Allen added her own playful animals and even a perky snail at the bottom to create this whimsical version of the scenic panels popular in mid-eighteenth-century Boston. Unusually well documented, this composition names Priscilla's parents, Benjamin and Elisabeth Allen, and an exact date, July 20, 1746. She worked tent stitches in crewel yarn on a twenty-two-thread-count canvas, adding French knots to make the sheep fluffy. H. 21"; W. 15 3/8".

Figure 28 (opposite). Detail of Plate 2, showing a vibrant, tent-stitched, canvas work representation of playful dogs.

Other sampler styles mirrored changes in the organization of needlework schools. When designs with buildings were popular, many samplers showed the school building at which the girl made her sampler. This sort of building housed a full-fledged boarding school, not a needle woman's family and some out-of-town, part-time students. As the number of boarding schools increased, so too did the number of samplers (most of these were made between 1800 and 1830), faithfully recording the institutions that produced them. Even if the name of the school were not stitched, certain distinguishing stylistic features might identify where a sampler was worked. For example, schools run by the Society of Friends often used a fine, vine-like wreath in their designs. True to the Quaker philosophy, these samplers showed meticulous workmanship and very conservative designs.

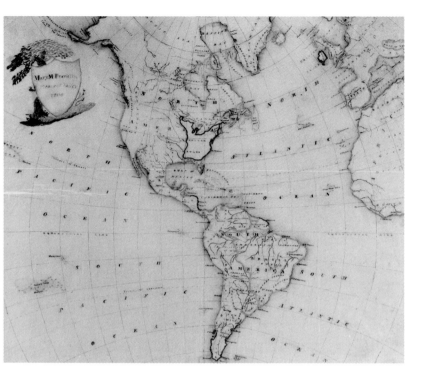

Figure 29. While maps were only moderately popular in America, the school that produced the largest number was a Quaker establishment in Pleasant Valley, New York. Using different map sources, some examples show both hemispheres, some North America, and some just part of the United States. Worked on lightweight, plain woven silk, Mary M. Franklin outlined the continents in black silk chenille yarns, and rivers in black silk thread. Water around the coastlines she painted blue; the tree behind the shield is green and brown chenille, and the names are stitched or drawn in black ink. Longitudinal lines are also drawn in ink. Completed in 1808. H. 20 3/8"; W. 23 3/4".

Figure 30. Both terrestrial and celestial globes were made at Westtown School. Ruth Wright of Exeter, Pennsylvania, made this terrestrial one there, sometime after her registration in October, 1814. The longitudinal lines are couched in blue silk, the tropics of Capricorn and Cancer in red silk, the Arctic and Antarctic circles and the continents in white silk. The continents and countries are outlined in white thread in a finely couched stitch. Dated 1815. Dia. 16".

Mary L. Browning

Wilmington Boarding School
1818

Figure 31. Reweavers today could not help but be impressed with Mary L. Browning's skill in 1818. On a linen ground she stitched nine different patterns, including the center one which imitates knitting. She worked all of the patches in cotton thread on linen ground, with her inscription in black silk. Apparently such fine darning was considered part of plain sewing in its day because the advertisements of the Quaker-run Wilmington (Delaware) Boarding School (for girls only) listed a well-rounded group of academic subjects but instruction only in "plain Needle work." H. 11 1/2"; W. 12". *Author's collection.*

By about 1800, the Quakers had begun to stress more academic education for girls, but they still required a perfect sampler of them.

DURING THE MID-EIGHTEENTH century the Quakers in Philadelphia offered academic education for girls. There were teachers of fine needlework, like Ann Marsh, who taught many of these young ladies their sewing skills. By late 1799, the Quakers, feeling that the city was not a safe or healthy place for young people, opened a boarding school called Westtown for both boys and girls, about twenty miles southwest of Philadelphia. Here, from the first, nearly equivalent educational courses were offered for both sexes, except that the girls took needlework and the boys more mathematics.

Molding the Accomplished Miss 65

Figure 32 (left). Samplers listing Sarah Stivours's school, like this one by Ruthey Putnam, even if not signed, are easily recognizable by their long, slanted satin stitches in crinkly silk and naively drawn figures and animals in cross stitch. Ruthey also used whip and French knots. She dated her Salem, Massachusetts example November the 27, 1778, in the 10th year of her age. The Salem minister, William Bentley, wrote of Sarah Stivours's funeral in 1790 that it, "was the best formed procession in testimony of respect to a private character which I have seen in Salem." *Gift of the Tenenbaum family in memory of Meyer Warren Tenenbaum.*

Figure 33 (top). A family history glued on the backboard says that eighteen-year-old Mary Jennison worked this piece in 1773 while attending a boarding school in Salem, Massachusetts, run possibly by Samuel Blythe and his wife. This versatile man was also a portrait painter, gilder, frame maker, teacher of drawing, and an organist. Who originated the use of long, often crinkly satin stitches in Salem-area work is arguable, but the popularity of this look continued for at least thirty years.. H. 8"; W. 13".

Figure 34 (bottom). Biblical scene on a black silk background of Joab slaying Absalom while Absalom's father, David, plays his harp, unaware that his son is dying. Absalom's hair is done with hair and the faces are painted. Stitches are satin, whip stitch, and French knots. Salem, Massachusetts, 1760–1785. H. 20 1/4"; W. 22".

Women who helped organize the Westtown school traveled to Ackworth, a Quaker school in the country south of Leeds, England, founded in 1779. Samplers brought back from the Ackworth School became models for the early Westtown pieces (figures 35 and 36).

Another fine, early school was the Moravian School in Bethlehem, Pennsylvania, founded in the early 1740s. Faced with dwindling enrollment from their own girls and pressured by requests from outsiders for admission, the church leaders opened the school to non-Moravian girls in 1786 (figure 37). Daughters from some of the most prominent families in America traveled great distances to attend. They represented Lees from Virginia; Sumpters, Hugers, and Alstons from South Carolina; Bayards and Elmendorfs from New Jersey; Bleeckers, Lansings, Livingstons, and Roosevelts from New York.

The school offered its students an exceptionally wide range of subjects for a girls' school of that era: reading, writing in English and German, arithmetic, geography, some history, a little botany, music, and drawing, plus intensive needlework training. A girl could enter the boarding school as young as age five or six and stay until she was sixteen. The range and extent of academic instruction here were more than a girl could get at any other school in the country. Most radical of all, this curriculum was scarcely different from the one Moravians offered boys (though in a separate school). The differences were that the girls were taught needlework and housekeeping. They could also learn spinning and weaving.

The town of Bethlehem became a popular stopping place for travelers interested in observing both the Moravian lifestyle in general and its superior educational system. A prime attraction was the superb and distinctive needlework produced and sold by both girl students and Moravian women. John Adams stopped in Bethlehem in 1777, and later wrote his wife, Abigail, about the visit. He described the fine water system that piped water to all parts of the town; the best grist, bolting, and fulling mills he had ever seen; and the industrious women who spun, wove, and were employed "in all the most curious [i.e., skillful] works in linen, wool, cotton, silver and gold, silk and velvet" (figures 38 and 39).[15]

Figure 35 (top). Mary Ann Clark of Woodbury, New Jersey, attended the Westtown School when she made this sampler, in 1812. She included an exceptional number of alphabets, each of the eight in a slightly different style as if she had copied them from a printer's handbook. Perhaps because of her proficiency in lettering, Mary was also allowed to include the stylized flowers—a symbol of achievement—associated with Friends' samplers. H. 16 3/4"; W. 19 3/4". *Author's collection.*

Figure 36 (bottom). Often these geometric designs, so typical of Quaker schools both here and in England, are used in conjunction with little flower sprigs such as in figure 35. Frances Pleasants of Philadelphia is identified as the maker because she was the only person with these initials at Westtown School in 1810. Worked entirely in blue silk cross stitch. H. 8 5/8"; W. 11 1/4". Photograph by L. Delmar Swan. *Author's collection.*

Figure 37. An 1836 lithograph by George Endicott shows the Moravian church and, in the right foreground, the young ladies' seminary at Bethlehem, Pennsylvania. *DMMC, WM, BX 8560/T97.*

Count Francesco dal Verme, an Italian who toured America in 1783 and 1784, also wrote of the needleworkers in Bethlehem: "They make very fine tambour embroidery." The tour of the town conveniently ended at the shop where handwork was sold, and the Count succumbed "to the custom of buying something, which everyone does who visits this place."[16]

The work of the girls was not always wholly their own. The pupils often paid teachers to add such finishing touches as supplying the backing or stiffening to pocketbooks and stitching them together. In some instances, the teachers also supplied the designs. A typical entry for expenses, from a teacher to a pupil, is the following, from Sister Maria Rosina Schulze to Betsey Dorsey, dated June 12, 1800:

> *Betsey Dorsey 1/2 yd Sattin for a framing Pice—8 [shillings] 6 [pence]*
> *drawing same —1 [shilling] 10 1/2 [pence]*
> *for making up a large Workbag—10 [shillings]*
> *making up Pincushions—1 [shilling] 6 [pence]*[17]

Figure 38 (top). Items to hold sewing aids, worked by Moravian pupils and teachers. At left is an oval, silk satin drawstring bag with decorative pin cushion attached to its front, worked in satin and whip stitches with three rows of wrapped silver thread couched down at intervals. The larger rectangle on the right has four flaps, opening out to hold the smaller envelope shape. Both are exquisitely worked on moiré silk in silk thread, ribbon, and crepe work, with a silk cord attached to the edge. Fine metal beads in groups of four are stitched to the edge of the smallest piece. A torn label says, "Wilkinson . . . Redhill," the latter a town near Bethlehem. The custom at Moravian schools was for the pupils to stitch the embroidered parts and the teacher to make them into objects. 1810–1820.
The rectangular cases are a gift of The Embroiderers' Guild of America, Inc.

Figure 39 (bottom). A circular mourning picture commemorating the death of Webster Downing, of Downington, Pennsylvania. On the stretcher is "MSD 1819" for Mary Downing who attended the Moravian school at Lititz. Teachers often moved among the schools at Bethlehem and Lititz, Pennsylvania, and at Salem, North Carolina, introducing their styles and the latest techniques. Chenille yarns are used for the ground, a stylized satin stitch for trees and hills, and whip stitch for clothes. Unusually well painted figures and faces. Diameter 19 3/4".

The Moravian philosophy of education stressed gentleness and compassion, both in and out of the classroom. The teachers, or sisters, as they were called, were devoted to their charges. During an age when birthdays were customarily almost ignored, these sisters celebrated their pupils' birthdays with "love feasts," complete with a small present for the honored girl. Likewise, the Moravians celebrated Christmas joyously while most of the rest of eighteenth-century society observed it soberly, if at all.

To discipline the students, the Moravians would go only so far as to consign a disobedient child to the "unfriendly bench." The authorities threatened incorrigibles with expulsion, but according to records, used that extreme only once. By contrast, in boarding schools, sewing classes, and dame schools, corporal punishment was common. For minor infractions, the teacher might deliver a thump on the head with a thimbled finger. A more serious transgression might merit that the offender stand blindfolded in the corner, balanced on a stool. Short-tempered instructors used switches.

While the Moravian schoolgirl was being intellectually cultivated and spiritually encouraged, the student at a typical girls' boarding school was learning the traditional female traits of docility, obedience, and graceful deportment. Teachers insisted that the girls sit with straight backs and heads held high while they studied or sewed. A staymaker, John McQueen, advertised in the *New York Mercury* for April 14, 1766, that he sold just the implement to encourage this discipline: "neat polished Steel Collars, very much worn by the young ladies in England, especially in Boarding Schools." A Wilmington, Delaware, teacher devised a cheaper method. She strung burrs on a tape and tied it around the student's neck.

At many schools it was standard practice for the headmistress to evaluate each girl's school progress and deportment in front of her classmates. At Miss Pierce's School, in Litchfield, Connecticut, the headmistress reviewed the girls each Saturday. In 1802, student Lucy Sheldon recorded these weekly ordeals in a diary, which she, like many girls, was encouraged to keep to note her accomplishments and her shortcomings. She wrote that Miss Pierce "had seen no fault in me except holding my arms stiff, which made me appear awkward." The next week Lucy could write," . . . [she] found no fault."[18]

The headmistress in the boarding school took responsibility for every aspect of a girl's training (figure 40). Miss Pierce, an early advocate of physical exercise for young ladies, required her girls to take lengthy walks regularly. (By contrast, John Adams had found the Moravian women pale and unhealthy in appearance, probably from being confined in their efficiently heated but excessively warm rooms.) Miss Pierce also believed it was her duty to guide her students toward a Christian life. She continually conjured up the horrors of dying unrepentant and urged her students not to delay repenting since they might die at any moment. Attendance at church each Sunday was required of the girls, and most of them diligently recorded in their diaries the theme of the sermon and the readings from the Bible presented during the service.

Boarding schools offered classes in character development, needlework and other accomplishments as well as academic subjects, all under one roof. If the parents could afford it, boarding school education made a considerable advance over the one-subject classes. At boarding school, a girl was likely to attend classes more regularly, stay for a longer time, and learn more. Whereas previously she would have been lucky to advance academically beyond the rudiments of dame school, at boarding school she received both a basic academic education and expanded training in female accomplishments (figure 41).

As eighteenth-century society grew wealthier, girls were taught an ever increasing array of accomplishments. It began in the sewing schools, where a teacher would expand her curriculum of needlework or needlework-related techniques. Throughout the eighteenth century, painting and drawing became increasingly important to needlework; pictures done by re-

Figure 41. A picture from an advertisement for the Andalusia Boarding School in Bucks County, Pennsylvania, The text lauded its healthy environment, far from Philadelphia and its periodic yellow fever epidemics. For $125 per year, headmistress Lucretia Chapman offered bed, board, washing, and a large range of academic subjects plus plain and ornamental needlework. French and piano cost $50 more, dancing $10. Her advertising stopped abruptly in June, 1831, when the school suddenly closed after the mysterious murder of her husband. At the trial, Pennsylvania's first for arsenic poisoning, Lucretia was accused but acquitted of spiking her husband's soup. *Courtesy, Kathleen Epstein.*

Figure 42. A quill work sconce made an impressive piece of handiwork, to be hung on the wall in the home of its maker and be seen by prospective suitors. Sconces such as this were usually made of tiny rolled cones of colored paper, wax animals, and shells, then sprinkled with mica to catch the candlelight. A family history attributes this sconce, one of a pair, to Elizabeth Wendell of Boston before her marriage in 1733. Variations of this technique remained popular through most of the eighteenth century. H 30 7/8"; W. 14 1/2".

verse painting on glass were very popular household ornaments. Mary M'Callister in the *Pennsylvania Gazette* of June 4, 1767, advertised that she taught young ladies the arts of "Painting on Glass, Japanning with Prints, Wax and Shell Work in the newest and most elegant Taste" as well as needlework. She was also one of the very rare teachers who taught "Pastry" making, one day a week.

The "Japanning with Prints" resembles modern decoupage work.

Shell and wax work and quilling (see Glossary) also found much favor with young ladies from the late seventeenth century through the third quarter of the eighteenth (figure 42). By the end of the century, parts of many embroidered pictures—faces, sky, and water—were painted on the same silk ground on which the pictures were also embroidered. In the *South Carolina Gazette* for January 30, 1753, John Thomas offered to "undertake to teach about six young ladies to draw and shade with *Indian* ink pencil, which may not only serve as an amusement to their genius, but in some respects become serviceable to them in needlework." In other words, learning to draw and shade in pencil would have helped these girls to design pictures or to highlight their silk embroideries.

John and Hamilton Stevenson, limners from Charleston, South Carolina, announced their drawing academy in the *South Carolina Gazette* of December 19, 1774. They offered to teach "Painting from the Life in Crayons and in Miniature on Ivory; Painting on Silk, Sattin, &c. Fan Painting together with the Art of working Designs in Hair upon Ivory, &c." (figure 43).

French was another eighteenth-century subject that enhanced the image of accomplished ladies. Charleston schools offered it as early as 1739. Because the city conducted important trade with the French West Indies, men learned French to expedite their business. Young ladies learned it to expedite their business of attracting men. After the Revolution, French became more popular in other large cities of America, spurred by our close ties with France.

All this training in skills and languages aimed at transforming a young girl into an "Accomplished Miss," as one schoolgirl, Eliza Southgate, called herself.[19] As the society grew wealthier and the boarding schools more elegant, the levels of sophistication that wealthy young ladies were called upon to demonstrate escalated. In 1853, one girl, Mary Service Steen of Philadelphia, felt unnerved at having to carry this worldly image. She wrote in her diary:

> *I often wished I was sixteen; it seemed to me as if that time*
> *would never arrive but now when I have reached that venerable*
> *age I wish I was only one half of it. I dislike the idea of getting*

A VIEW OF NEW YORK DONE BY MARY BOWEN IN THE 10TH YEAR OF HER AGE 1807

Figure 43. An embroidered picture stitched by ten-year-old Mary Bowen at Mrs. Lockwood's boarding school in New Jersey. She copied from an 1801 engraving by William Rollinson, in turn based on a view by John Wood entitled "New York from Long Island." The ships and far buildings are stitched in tiny black seed and whip stitches (of either hair or silk) to imitate stipple engraving. Such work was called print work. Most print works are worked in black stitches; this one is unusual because the foreground is in colors. The original frame and black reverse painted glass mat have a piece of the *New Jersey Journal* (Elizabeth, New Jersey) for March 24, 1807, glued to the back. Needlework only: H. 13 1/8"; W. 19 7/16".

any older very much And to think of leaving school is the thing I
like least of all. This happens to be my last year as a school girl.
I suppose I will have to become very prim & precise; and in case I
should not recollect or indeed not know anything about what a
person is saying, I will have to appear as if I did, because I am a
"finished lady," while now I am still a school girl I can show my
ignorance if I choose.[20]

Mary was not alone in suspecting that a "finished lady" was little
more than an ignorant schoolgirl with a lot of accomplishments. At the end
of the eighteenth century, reformers began to charge that the boarding
schools had become frivolous and impractical, and their graduates the same.
Dr. William Buchan wrote, "A great part of the time [is] inconsiderately
spent by young ladies in fancy works, and in learning to draw, to paint, or
to play upon some musical instrument, of which they will never feel the
want." In Buchan's view, these girls were appallingly lacking in what they
needed to know to be competent wives and mothers, and he suggested that
they be trained in this field like any tradesman was in his. Buchan observed, "It is common to see women, who are supposed to have had a very
genteel education, so ignorant, when they come to have children, of everything with which a mother ought to be acquainted, that the infant itself is as
wise as the parent."[21]

Hannah More, a conservative Englishwoman who did believe in better education for girls, wrote in *The Lady's Pocket Library,* published in Philadelphia in 1792, " . . . ornamental Accomplishments will but indifferently
qualify a woman to perform the *duties* of life, though it is highly proper she
should possess them" for amusement.[22]

These were the voices of moderation. They saw nothing wrong with
the basic aim of the boarding schools, that of preparing a girl for marriage.
They charged only that the schools had strayed from their purpose. Get
back to basics, they advised. Dr. Benjamin Rush said, in criticism of teaching
instrumental music to girls, "After they become mistress of families, their
harpsichords serve only as side-boards for their parlours."[23]

As if to reinforce the charges of the critics, the needlework skills of
some of the girls in boarding schools were becoming less expert. Beulah
Purinton's showy 1812 sampler (plate 9) demonstrates this gradual decline.

Her green wool and linen background displays an attractive composition, but close examination reveals long, sloppy stitchery.

Some commentators went further than criticizing simply the performance of the schools. They attacked the very principle on which many boarding schools were founded. This was a time during which some women were taking very seriously the Revolution's rhetoric of equality—so seriously, in fact, as to question the basic assumption that girls should be denied the academic training available to boys. To them the boarding schools were an abomination.

In July, 1791, in the *Universal Asylum and Columbian Magazine*, an article "By a Lady" (who evidently did not consider it yet propitious to publish her name) scathingly reviewed "the future education of girls." The article described a system in which girls were "committed to illiterate teachers, and as illiterate school-mistresses . . . are cooped up in a room, confined to needle-work, deprived of exercises, reproved without being faulty, and schooled in frivolity."[24]

Eliza Southgate wrote, "I found the mind of a female, if such a thing existed, was thought not worth cultivation." Later, she added, "Do you suppose the mind of a woman the only work of God that was made in vain?" Of a Mrs. Wyman, whose school she had attended, Eliza said, "she treated me as her own malicious heart dictated." However, Eliza had nothing but praise for a Mrs. Rowson, the headmistress at the second school Eliza tried. She wrote her younger sister, who was then a student at Mrs. Rowson's, "You must allow that no woman was ever better calculated to govern a school than Mrs. Rowson. She governs by the love with which she inspires her scholars."[25]

If all the fancy needlework and extra frills made for a frivolous education, not many of the girls seemed to mind as long as the schoolmistress treated them kindly. Sarah Emery remembered fondly, "Miss Emerson was a most accomplished needle woman, inducting her pupils into mysteries of ornamental marking and embroidery. This fancy work opened a new world of delight."[26]

In any case, the criticisms of the boarding schools prompted the establishment of academies, or seminaries, for girls. Some of these institutions

Figure 44. A view of Emma Willard's Female Seminary in Troy, New York, from a woodcut published in 1841 in *Historical Collections of the State of New York* by John Barber. *Courtesy, Kathleen Epstein.*

used the new label but provided no real academic improvements. However, other schools made a genuine attempt to raise the standards. A few, such as the Deerfield Academy in Massachusetts, were even coeducational early in the nineteenth century. In 1799, Deerfield Academy opened for both boys and girls who could read. It cost two dollars per quarter. Drawing was twenty-five cents more and needlework instruction an additional twenty-five cents. Boarding, if needed, was extra. Later the academy was open only for boys.[27] In 1821, persistent Emma Willard started the Troy Female Seminary (figure 44) with four thousand dollars she obtained from taxes raised by the city of Troy, New York. Gradually, a combination of private money and public support helped such seminaries as the Georgia Female College in Macon and Mary Lyon's Mount Holyoke Academy to raise their course offerings up to college level.

Even as women's education advanced, however, most girls continued to attend school to be groomed to win a husband and properly prepare to be his wife. The production of accomplished misses did not abate, though it did change somewhat to accommodate its critics by reemphasizing practical homemaking and providing training that was more academic. Following the lead of such eighteenth-century commentators as Dr. Rush, some nineteenth-century educators merged the idea of improved education for women with an already-conceived role for women as housewives. In his 1787 examination address to the Young Ladies Academy of Philadelphia, Rush had preached:

> I know that the elevation of the female mind, by means moral, physical, and religious truth, is considered by some men as unfriendly to the domestic character of a woman. But this is the prejudice of little minds, and springs from the same spirit which opposes the general diffusion of knowledge among the citizens [men] of our republic. If men believe that ignorance is favourable to the government of the female sex, they are certainly deceived; for a weak and ignorant woman will always be governed with the greatest difficulty. . . . It will be in your power, LADIES, to correct the mistakes and practices of our sex upon these subjects, by demonstrating that the female temper can only be governed by reason.[28]

The issue was not whether to become a housewife and mother—that much was assumed—but how to be the most capable wife and mother. By the mid-nineteenth century, housewifery was on its way to becoming not just the expected occupation of a woman, but an exalted position for her. In 1841, Catherine Beecher, who had attended Miss Pierce's school and later opened her own school (it became the Hartford Female Seminary), wrote in A *Treatise on Domestic Economy*, "The proper education of a man decides the welfare of an individual; but educate a woman and the interests of the

Plate 4 (overleaf). . One wonders if Nabby Fitch, who finished her solidly worked sampler in 1766, found her stiff, stylized apple tree and pitchfork-like tulips amusing. Both features are seen in a few other early Norwich, Connecticut, pieces although not necessarily solidly worked. The bottom line states, "Nabby Fitch her sampler made in the 9th year of her age." She used cross, double cross, tent, Queen's, and eyelet stitches. H. 10"; W. 10 1/2". *Author's collection.*

Plate 5 (left). "Elizabeth Richards Ended her Sampler in the 10th Year of her Age January the 10th." This picture panel is worked in the same manner and contains all the elements as the 1745–1755 Boston canvas work pictures. The inheritor of an almost identical sampler (see Ethel Standwood and Eva Coe, *American Samplers*, plate xxxviii) told the author that Zebiah Gore made hers in 1791. Contemporaries, these girls undoubtedly had the same teacher. Elizabeth used cross stitch for the upper panel, tent stitch for the picture, real hair on the people, bullion stitches for the lambs, and satin stitches for facial details. The letters and verse are in cross stitch, the border in eyelet. H. 17 1/2"; W. 14 3/4". *Gift of H. Rodney Sharp.*

Plate 6 (right). One of a pair of bird pictures worked by Sarah Wistar, a fourteen-year-old Philadelphian, in 1752. A piece of wool flannel was found under the silk; it served to shield the embroidery from the wooden backboard and pad it slightly. H. 9 1/2"; W. 7".

whole family are secured."[29]

Thus, homemaking evolved from a dutiful performance of chores to a calling in which a woman could find fulfillment by creating a haven-like home for her family. Catherine Beecher, while glorifying the mid-nineteenth-century housewife, also gave practical advice on the best methods of accomplishing wifely tasks. Her advocacy of sensible, systematic home-making helped generate a movement for better female education and training in food preparation, health, nutrition, and household management. This culminated in the start of home economics training in public schools. Doctors Rush and Buchan would have been pleased.

Yet even as housewifery gained respectability and women were lauded for possessing "superior moral values," they could not escape being treated as second-rate intellects. As late as 1873, reformer and feminist Abba Goold Woolson took the young ladies' schools to task for the poor quality of the education they offered. In the chapter "The Accomplishments" in her book *Woman in American Society*, Woolson pleaded that girls be freed from "the fancy-work which now engrosses their time and disfigures our parlor-walls and mantels." Needlework and "gewgaws," as she termed the other types of ornamental work, were "produced at the expense of the eyesight, the health, and intelligence of [our] daughters."[30]

At the start of the nineteenth century, Eliza Southgate recognized the intellectually stale life in store for her as a woman. In a letter to her male cousin she observed, "The business and pursuits of men require deep thinking, judgment, and moderation, while, on the other hand, females are under no necessity of dipping deep, but merely 'skim the surface.'" When she had finished her schooling, Eliza mused about "what profession I should choose were I a man." She even went so far as to question the necessity for a girl to be married. She wrote,

> I do not esteem marriage absolutely essential to happiness. . . . A single life is considered too generally a reproach; but let me ask you, which is the more despicable—she who marries a man she scarcely thinks well of—to avoid the reputation of an old maid . . . [or she who has] wisdom enough to despise so mean a sacrifice to the opinion of the rabble."

Figure 45 (opposite). A fashionable Federal-style piano for a young lady. This one has an inlaid, painted, mahogany and satinwood case. The instrument was made in New York City between 1804 and 1814 by John Geib and Son.

But even such a rebel as Eliza Southgate learned to play by the rules. In 1800, she bought an imported piano for $150, though she admitted she had little musical talent (figure 45). Then she settled in to "patiently . . . wait till some clever fellow shall take a fancy to me and place me in a situation. I am determined to make the best of it, let it be what it will."[31]

While a girl waited for "some clever fellow," she filled her dowry chest with all the necessities for a well-run household, including quilts, bed rugs, and the finest linens she could make (see Glossary). As she was thus busily engaged with her needle, she presented a demure, enticing female figure. Indeed the postures and attitudes of fine sewing exemplified the ideal woman—relaxed and at leisure, posturing prettily, her hands dutifully occupied, showing her industry. The stitches might have been difficult, but not to the extent that they commanded a girl's full attention. A girl kept her eyes downcast, on work in hand, but her ears and mind were open to the man paying court. She needed to be busy, so as not to appear too eager to be wooed; but doing fancy needlework was a pretty business, meant to encourage a suitor. In short, fancy needlework could be a sexual lure, a female ploy in the courtship game.

The sampler verse suggested by one father in the May, 1784, *Boston Magazine* put it succinctly, if discreetly:

> *And Man acknowledges, in all his pride,*
> *Needles attract, when our fair fingers guide.*

Gilbert Stuart caught this display of stylized femininity in his portrait of two young girls doing tambour work (plate 10). Sitting properly and gracefully erect, dressed luxuriously, and projecting the intelligence of accomplished ladies, these girls seem to invite a discreet flirtation. Certainly their needlework is not distracting them.

During the seventeenth century, when parental domination was more absolute, parents selected a mate for their child and made all the arrangements, such as provisions for a dowry and other financial matters. Usually the child did have the right to refuse to marry the parents' choice. By the eighteenth century, the selection of a mate was still made by the parents, but also sometimes by the young people themselves; however, there were few places for the youth of rural areas to meet and to socialize. Church

services, occasional barn raisings, and quilting bees provided some opportunity, but most of it was hit-or-miss casual contact. In towns and cities, the parents arranged tight little social gatherings, such as tea parties, picnics, and fishing parties.

A socially acceptable method of bringing both sexes together was the dancing class. Although Puritan New England prohibited dancing until the first part of the eighteenth century and the Quakers in the middle colonies also frowned upon dancing as a frivolity, the rest of the colonies had no such inhibitions. In the New York area, even in the seventeenth century, boys and girls of wealthy families attended dancing classes. These classes eventually developed into even more structured and formal "dancing assemblies."

Once a young man and woman expressed an interest in each other, the fathers discussed financial arrangements. Generally, the boy's father was expected to provide about twice as much money or property as the girl's, but in areas where women outnumbered men, such as in late eighteenth-century Massachusetts, Rhode Island, and Connecticut, the bargaining was of little benefit to the girl. A young man visited his bride-to-be after the girl's father gave his permission for courtship. Often the suitor had to travel great distances on foot, and under such circumstances a long courtship was not the rule.

The man played the aggressor, of course, in this ritual. The woman appeared passive, modest, and virtuous (industrious), for which needlework was the perfect prop. In 1707, in *Instructions for the Education of a Daughter*, English author F. Fenelon wrote, "beware of the Reputation of being *Witty*, ... A Maid ought not speak but for necessity.... That which pleases in her is her Silence, her Modesty, her love of Retirement ... her Industry for Works of Embroidery and fine Needle-Work."[32]

In an article reprinted in 1792 in *The Lady's Pocket Library* from his *Legacy to his Daughters*, English physician Dr. John Gregory added this advice:

> *It is a maxim laid down among you, and a very prudent one it is, that love is not to begin on your part.... [H]e contracts an attachment to you. When you perceive it, it excites your gratitude:*

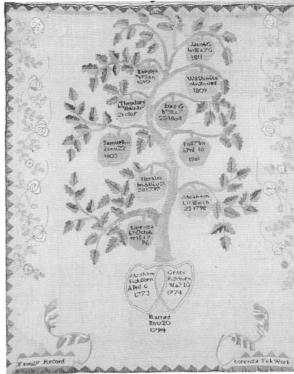

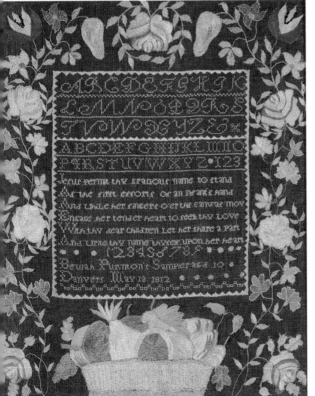

Plate 7 (above left). Mary King signed this skillfully done silk embroidery in 1754. On a gold-colored silk moiré ground, she worked a sophisticated tree of life, accenting it with glass beads and detailing it with metallic thread. Mary used satin and surface satin, whip, seed, and couching stitches for her masterpiece. H. 18 1/4"; W. 24 1/8".

Plate 8 (above right). Genealogical sampler by Lorenza Fisk, daughter of Grace and Abraham Fisk of Waltham, Massachusetts. Worked on a linen ground with silk yarn in satin, whip, tent, flat, cross, and chain. H. 18 3/4"; W. 16 1/2". *Gift of Mrs. Alfred C. Harrison.*

Plate 9 (left) Between 1785 and 1825 a small number of American samplers were worked on colored grounds. Most used green or brown grounds; blue and red are rare. Several of the green grounds tested by the author, including this one, prove to be linen warps and wool wefts. "Beulah Purinton's Sampler ag'd 10 Danvers [Mass.] May 13, 1812" is cross-stitched in silk yarns. She used a crinkled silk with satin, whip, French knots, and eyelet stitches for the fruit basket and surrounding flowering vine. H. 19 1/2"; W. 15 1/4".

Plate 10 (following). Painting of Miss Vick and her cousin, Miss Foster, by Gilbert Stuart. Miss Vick is doing tambour work while her cousin holds the pattern As they did tambour work, young ladies could present themselves in graceful, beguiling poses. Painted between 1787 and 1792. *Owned by Philip and Charlotte Hanes.*

Molding the Accomplished Miss 87

this gratitude rises into a preference: . . . If you love him, let me advise you never to discover to him the full extent of your love, no, not although you marry him. . . . . Violent love cannot subsist, at least cannot be expressed for any time together on both sides . . . [without] satiety and disgust.[33]

Now this was a very delicate set of feelings to manage: gratitude rising to a preference but not to anything so dangerous as love. A girl had to know her protocol; propriety itself depended on it. Eliza Southgate implied it could all be rather trying for a miss, trained as she had been to devote herself to a man, yet unable to express it openly before he authorized it by asking her to marry. Eliza wrote, "I would strain every nerve and rouse every faculty to quell the first appearance [of love]. . . . I could never love without being loved."[34]

There was plenty of instruction for misses on the theme of keeping up one's guard against suitors. In 1837, *The Young Lady's Friend* advised, "Never join in any rude plays that will subject you to being kissed or handled in any way by gentlemen. Do not suffer your hand to be held or squeezed, without showing that it displeases you by instantly withdrawing it."[35]

In his *Annals of Philadelphia . . . and Reminiscences of New York City*, John Fanning Watson gives us a glimpse of how this elaborate courtship ritual actually worked. Writing around 1846, Watson was by this time a senior citizen who looked back bemused on one old courtship scene. He tells of a husband smoking his pipe while his wife,

in her chintz dress and mob cap, was at his side, engaged in making patchwork; whilst lovely Prudence sat quite erect by her mama, with her pincushion and house-wife [i.e., a pocket, see figure 60] dangling from her waist, and her eyes cast down, diligently pricking her fingers instead of her sampler. Courting was sober business in old times. [The beau] showed his affection very properly by keeping at a respectful distance. He passed the evening in talking politics and the scarcity of money with his future father-in-law; in assisting his future mother-in-law to arrange her party-coloured squares; in picking up balls of yarn, as they were respectively dropped by the maiden aunts; now and then casting sly sheep's eyes at Prudence, at every instance of which

familiarity the aforesaid maiden ladies dropped a stitch! As soon
as the bell rung nine, he gave one tender squint at [Prudence] and
took his leave.[36]

One hopes that the scene itself was not quite as precious as the account of it. In any case, the American girls who engaged in these courtship rituals were freewheeling compared to their European counterparts. In 1822, Frances Wright, the English visitor who wrote *Views of Society and Manners in America*, said, "The liberty enjoyed by the young women often occasions some surprise to foreigners." She described American young women as "marked by sweetness, artlessness, and liveliness. . . . [They have] a certain untaught grace and gaiety of the heart equally removed from the studied English coolness and indifference, and from the no less studied French vivacity and mannerism."[37]

That gentleman from Savannah who advertised for a mate could hardly have asked for more.

NOTES

1. Lockridge, *Literacy*, 7, 77, 97. Sicherman, "American History," 467. Diary of Elizabeth Drinker, January 15, 1799.
2. Emery, *Reminiscences*, 221.
3. Sigourney, "Schoolmistress," 295.
4. Samuel Sewall to Edward Hull. March 28, 1687, and Samuel Sewall to David Allen. March 28, 1687, "Letter-Book of Samuel Sewall," 44.
5. Winslow, *Diary of Anna Green Winslow*, 17.
6. Kathleen Epstein, personal communication, 1994. *A Stitch Through Time*, exhibit, The Textile Museum, Washington, D. C., May 27–October 16, 1994.
7. Inventory of Elizabeth Brunson, April 26, 1694, 414.
8. Swan, "Recent Discoveries," 1334–1343.
9. Emery, *Reminiscences*, 21.
10. Wister., *Sally Wister's Journal*, 159. Betty Ring, *Girlhood Embroidery*, vol. II, 337, fig. 354
11. Gilman, *Recollections*, 10–11.
12. Livingston. *Nancy Shippen*, 43.
13. Olney Winsor to his wife, February 22, 1787.
14. Benes, "Decorated Family Records," 93–94.
15. Adams, *Familiar Letters*, 240–42.
16. Cometti, *Seeing America*, 32.
17. Account of Betsey Dorsey.
18. Vanderpoel, *Chronicles*, 46. For a recent in-depth discussion of Mrs. Pierce's school, see Theodore and Nancy Sizer, Sally Schwager, Lynne Templeton Brickley, and Glee Krueger. *To Ornament Their Minds: Sarah Pierce's Litchfield Female Academy, 1792–1833.* (Litchfield Historical Society, 1993).
19. Bowne, *Girl's Life*, 13.
20. Manuscript diary of Mary S. Steen. October 29. 1853.
21. Buchan, *Advice to Mothers*, 239, 236.
22. More, "Essays for Young Ladies," 53.
23. Rush, "Thoughts upon Female Education," 288.
24. By a Lady. "Supposed Superiority," 10.
25. Bowne, *Girl's Life*, 56, 60, 18, 31.
26. Emery, *Reminiscences*, 21
27. Flynt, *Ornamental and Useful Accomplishments*, 18.
28. Rush, "Thoughts upon Female Education, " 291–92.
29. Beecher, *Treatise on Domestic Economy*, 37.
30. Woolson. *Woman in American Society*, 53.
31. Bowne, *Girl's Life*, 59, 102, 38, 22.
32. Fenelon. *Instructions*, 208, 288.
33. Gregory. "Legacy," 107–10.
34. Bowne, *Girl's Life*, 41.
35. [Farrar], *Young Lady's Friend*, 293.
36. Watson, *Annals*, 214.
37. Wright, *Views of Society*, 391, 32.

3 The Golden Years of Needlework
The Age of Craftsmanship

Figure 46 (opposite).
Exquisitely designed and
executed crewel work in three
shades of blue. Fine crewel
yarns are stitched in an
unusually great variety of
stitches: flat, whip, back,
herringbone, seed, satin,
buttonhole, cross, and
weaving. Not in its original
form and quilted at a later
date. Massachusetts;
1740–1780. H. 90 1/2";
W. 96 1/4".

MOST OF THE finest needlework ever done in this country was produced by women of the more prosperous classes during the years between
1700 and 1780 . The techniques they used included canvas work, crewel
work, and lace work, much silk embroidery, and, late in the period, tambour
work. Most of these pieces were made to adorn an article of some sort,
whether clothing, an everyday accessory such as a pocket or pocketbook,
or—for the most ambitious needleworkers—a household furnishing. This
was an age in which enormous importance was attached to possessions, and
particularly household possessions because people spent much more time in
their homes than they do today.

A well-off man might occasionally leave his home on business, but
colonial times had nothing to rival the transience of today's businessman.
Most businesses were situated near if not in or adjacent to the home, and a
man's commercial dealings rarely took him far away. Even a prosperous
man was not likely to travel farther from his home than to a local inn or
tavern to discuss the issues of the day and to enjoy some simple entertainment.

Normally, a married woman would venture out of the house only to
attend church, to shop for the few household supplies she did not produce
herself, and to visit nearby friends and relatives. In general, it was not until
the last quarter of the eighteenth century that the ritualistic tea partying,
card playing, and other such lighthearted social intercourse became common
among women wealthy enough to have leisure time. Furthermore, whatever
socializing did take place during the seventeenth and eighteenth centuries
almost always occurred in the home. Since there were no restaurants and
little commercial entertainment, an afternoon or evening of recreation invariably meant visiting someone else's home or entertaining in one's own
home.

During the seventeenth century, especially in New England, most weddings were performed in the home, often by a civil authority such as a magistrate. As the eighteenth century progressed, ministers presided over weddings more frequently and more ceremonies took place in churches; however, the post-wedding celebrations not only remained in the home but grew more elaborate, fostering an even greater consciousness of the self and the home that one presented to others.

With the home being the hub of social activity as well as of family life, a family naturally sought to furnish it as impressively as possible. Because there were so few other indulgences and luxuries then available to the consumer for any amount of money, fine furnishings conveyed the level of one's prosperity and social standing far more strongly than they do today. In an era when travel for pleasure was almost unknown, professional entertainment almost nonexistent, and the range of tangible luxury items severely limited, home furnishings represented one of the few ways in which a thriving family could display its affluence.

Moreover, fine furnishings could be practical investments. A handsome piece of silver, for example, could serve not only as a useful item and an object of display but also as a form of money. Such a piece was likely to have been fashioned of silver coins that the family had entrusted to a silversmith to be melted down and reshaped into an artistic form. The resulting hollowware was a more secure way to keep one's silver than in coin since there were no banks during colonial times. A piece of hollowware usually carried its owner's initials and some identifying mark of the silversmith who made it; if lost or stolen, the piece was far more likely to be recovered. Silversmiths commonly kept a suspicious-looking piece if it was brought to them and then advertised for its owner, with a description of its marks.

Although not directly derived from currency, a piece of furniture could also represent an important investment for a wealthy family, and much time and consideration on the part of the head of the household would be given to the planning and overseeing of its creation. First, he would select a cabinetmaker and, in consultation with him, decide on the style of the piece, the woods to be used, the extent and placement of any carving or inlay work, and, of course, the price. Because fine furniture called

Plate 11 (overleaf). Easy chair, probably Boston, covered with Irish stitch canvas work in an outstanding example of the flame design, worked in crewels. Found in poor condition without a cushion. Usable needlework was probably removed from the back of he chair to make the cushion. America; 1720–1770. H. 46 7/8"; W. 35 1/2".

Plate 12 (above). A finely worked tent stitch slip seat, made specially for this chair by a member of the Bangs family of Newport, Rhode Island. This piece comes from a set of at least six, each with a slightly different design. The chairs marked IIII and VI are owned by Winterthur Museum; 1745–1785. H. 14 1/2"; W. 19 1/8".

Plate 13 (below). Irish-stitched slip seat with an alternating carnation and jagged oval pattern—one of the more difficult designs to execute. America; 1740–1790. H. 14 1/4"; W. 20".

Plate 14 (opposite) This pocketbook, worked with silk yarns, is one of the finest known canvas work examples. The embroiderer chose a superb color combination and artfully produced different textures with her choice of stitches. The blue-green background is done in tent stitches that cover two ground threads on a fifty-two-thread-count canvas The flowers, petals, stems, and leaves were worked over one thread, angling the stitches in the opposite direction. The rougher texture in the rose and bell-like flower on the flap comes from the cross stitch. Probably Philadelphia; 1740–1790. *Owned by the Chester County Historical Society.*

Plate 15. A cross-stitched pocketbook worked on canvas of fifty-two threads to the inch. The embroiderer chose to use crewel yarns and cover crossed pairs of threads with each stitch. A microscopic examination reveals reddish-brown inked pattern guidelines. America; 1740–1790. H. 7 1/4"; W. 4".

Figure 47. From a set of four known canvas chair seats, finely worked in tent stitch, depicting different scenes surrounded by similar flowered borders. Two of the seats are in the Winterthur Museum and two are in the Museum of Fine Arts, Boston. The one shown here portrays a couple en route to market, carrying milk and fowl. Winterthur Museum also owns a silk embroidery on a black satin background with the same scene. Boston; 1740–1760. H 19 1/2"; W. 23 1/4".

for a fine room in which to display them, he would also require the services of a carpenter, a painter, and—for fashionable paneling and molding—a carver and possibly a gilder.

Fancy needlework represented a woman's contribution to the beauty of the family's possessions. A bride brought to her new home stitched canvas or crewel-embroidered chair covers designed for the particular style of each piece (plate 11). Few wives had the opportunity to do such time-consuming projects after marriage. Some of these coverings were so well cared for and wore so well that they are still displayed on the furniture today (plates 12 and 13; figure 47).

The wives' needlework did not go unappreciated, for like young women's samplers, pieces made for the home earned the praise and attention of all. For example, in his 1782 will, John Morris of Southwark, Pennsylvania, bequeathed to his grandson "8 Mahogany Chairs the Seats of which were worked by his Mother." In 1820, another man, George Y. Cutler, reflected in his diary that when he had been a child, his mother and aunt "used chairs . . . which were 'worked' on the seat by their own hands. . . . [A] great deal of labor was bestowed upon [these chair seats] & . . . valuable and fashionable they were."[1]

Although it is impossible to tell precisely what sorts of chair seats these men were referring to, most of the chair coverings surviving from this period are pieces of canvas work (see Glossary; plate 13). Often called needlepoint today, the appeal of canvas work to American women has always been strong. Unlike crewel embroidery, which apparently was seldom, if ever, done in the South, canvas work was done in all the colonies during the seventeenth and eighteenth centuries. This colonial canvas work is characterized by four stitches: the tent stitch, the cross stitch, the Irish stitch, and the Queen's stitch (see Glossary). The tent stitch progresses slowly, and before the twentieth century a needle worker could badly distort her canvas with it, since she worked it in horizontal rows. It has, however, always been an excellent stitch for defining an intricate design. Occasionally, canvas workers used it in making pocketbooks, but it appears most often in work with detailed scenic or floral designs, such as the fishing lady needlework pictures done in the Boston area during the mid-eighteenth century. The schoolgirls who worked these pictures did them almost entirely in tent stitch, usually on canvas with crewel or silk yarns. The chair seat in figure 47 shows elements of the fishing lady pictures. Whether a schoolgirl or a more mature embroiderer did this particular piece, the maker obviously borrowed liberally from the tent-stitched needlework designs being done in Boston sewing schools.

Since tent-stitched canvas work had a richness about it that reminded some people of the expensive and desirable loom-woven European tapestries, this particular needlework form was occasionally called tapestry work. For instance, a Margaret Taitail advertised in the *Boston Evening-Post* of April 23, 1739, that she taught "all sorts of Needle Work Tapestry, Em-

broidery, and Marking" (plate 14).

Although women had learned how to cross-stitch by marking their household goods and the family wardrobe, they rarely used the cross stitch in canvas work because it was coarser than tent stitch (plate 16). Only when cross stitch was worked over single threads of a fine canvas (plate 15) could it rival the tent stitch in depiction of details.

The Queen's stitch was the most difficult and time-consuming of all the canvas work stitches. Because even fine crewel yarns were apt to fuzz and obscure the intricate nature of the stitch, the Queen's stitch was almost always worked in silk yarns. Usually it was limited to small items such as pocketbooks, sewing purses, pinballs, and pincushions (figures 48 and 49).

The Irish stitch was by far the most common canvas work stitch used during the seventeenth and eighteenth centuries if we are to judge by the number of written references and surviving pieces. No doubt its appeal

Figure 48 (left). A detail of the Queen's stitch worked on canvas in silk yarns. From a sewing case made by Beulah Biddle in 1783. Probably Philadelphia.
H. 4 3/4"; W. 4 1/8".

Figure 49 (right). Pinballs worked in the Queen's stitch. One bears an attached chain, by which it hung at the waist from a chatelaine. Handmade pins and a silver needle holder. America; 1760–1800.
H. 2 1/4"; W. 2".

lay in how rapidly it progressed and its facility, for it covered, vertically, four threads of the canvas rather than a single thread, as in the tent stitch.

Especially between 1740 and 1790, the Irish stitch was the favorite stitch for pocketbooks (plates 17 and 18) though few were worked in tent stitch (plate 14).[2] These small, envelope-shaped holders served as portable bank safe-deposit boxes (banks did not exist at this time) and enabled people to carry their valuables with them. Men used pocketbooks to carry currency, promissory notes, deeds, wills, and other important papers that they might not want to leave in a secret compartment in a piece of furniture (plate 18). Women, who seldom dealt with legal documents, used their pocketbooks for jewelry, sewing items, and other trinkets.

The Irish stitch was also used for chair seats, the upholstery of easy chairs, wall pockets, pincushions, book covers, fire screens, and even table-cloths (plates 19, 20, and 21). A fire screen, when placed between the fire-place and a chair, allowed one to sit close to a fire for warmth and yet be shielded from intense heat. Sarah Emery described one of these devices and its needlework embellishment as "an elegantly embroidered fire-screen, with mahogany frame, that could be raised or lowered at pleasure."[3] Hand-held fire screens (figure 50) served the same purpose less conveniently but less expensively and were considered important for the protection of a woman's complexion.

On May 9, 1760, Elizabeth Drinker mentioned a fire screen covered in "Irishstitched Flowers." This is a rare and difficult use of the Irish stitch but Elizabeth had surely been up to the task; she had been fortunate enough to attend Anthony Benezet's school for young women, which was the finest academic school of its day. Her diary starts in 1757 by listing ninety nee-dlework projects she subsequently completed by early 1761, this fire screen being one of them. Since she was unmarried at this time and her parents were deceased, Elizabeth was probably paid to work these items. Most of these pieces were small: "round Pincushons," "a Queen Stitch cover for Polly's twezer case," or an "Irishstich Tea Kittle holder." However, some were more substantial and more time-consuming, such as "a large Woosted Bible Cover."[4] With such an advanced repertoire in needlework, it is very likely she had also attended Ann Marsh's school. On May 3, 1784, she chose

Figure 50 A shield-shaped hand-held fire screen of Irish-stitched canvas work in shades of red, yellow, blue, brown, and black. America; 1740–1780. H. 17 1.4"; W 11 1/2".

Ann Marsh to be her daughter's teacher; "Molly began a quarter at A Marshs School—first of her going there."

Ann Flowers and Elizabeth Drinker were contemporary Philadelphians and probably students at the same school. Fortunately a varied group of items made by Ann Flowers still exists. Just before her marriage, Ann worked Irish stitched flowers on the side panels of a prayer book cover dated 1765 (figure 51). She also embroidered a small silk-on-silk coat of arms with accents of metal-wrapped thread, still in its original deep Philadelphia-style frame (figure 52). Ann's sister, Mary, worked an identical piece except that she used scarlet threads behind the shield instead of pale gold. Undated, but undoubtedly older than the coat of arms, is a rare survival, a handmade drawing book with Ann's and Mary's names on the front (figure 53). Unfinished is a Philadelphia compartmented sampler.[5] The similarity of this sampler to Mary Cooper's (figure 103) suggests that the two girls worked their samplers in the same school. A fifth item is a one-piece quilt with a silk top and a mid-eighteenth-century French block printed backing signed "Ann Flowers."[6]

Another woman whose needlework survives in remarkable quantity is Mary Alsop, nee Wright, of Middletown, Connecticut (plate 22). She was born in 1740, married in 1760 to Richard Alsop, gave birth to ten children, eight of whom lived beyond infancy, but was widowed by 1776. Before his death, Richard had become a successful merchant, landowner, and legislator. At his death, Mary assumed the unusual role for females of her day of administratrix of her husband's large estate, which took fourteen years to settle. Meanwhile, she continued to carry on many of his former interests, and the family continued to prosper.

Mary Alsop's premarital needlework is remarkable; she attended Sarah Osborn's school in Newport, Rhode Island, in 1754.[7] A small tent stitched picture entitled "SPRING" and initialed "M W" and another that says "SUMMER" survive in their original frames along with another untitled, similar piece. Before marriage she produced a cross stitched roundabout chair seat, or corner chair, in a floral design signed in fine tent stitch "Molly Wright;" a floral, tent stitched pocketbook naming her father, Joseph Wright; and a Queen's stitch silk pocketbook for herself in 1758. Listed in

Figure 51 (left). In 1765, the year of Ann Flower's marriage, both she and her father, formerly Quakers, became Episcopalians for a time. This rare example of "Irish stitch flowers" (Elizabeth Drinker's term) covers a *Book of Common Prayer* published in London in 1758. To work this difficult piece , Ann used fine crewel yarns on a linen foundation of forty-two threads per inch. The background is dark blue with rose and blue flowers tied with a rose bow. The spine is worked in cross stitch with Ann's name and date in silk.
H. 7"; W. 4 1/2"; D. 3".

Figure 52 (right). An accurate representation of the Flowers family arms, delicately embroidered on cream moiré silk ground. Satin, couching, and outline stitches in greens, brown, and rose with metallic thread used for the cipher and unicorns' tails. The body of the upper unicorn is raised by padding. Original, deep Philadelphia-type frame with old script on the back, "Ann Flower 1763."

Figure 53. A page from Ann and Mary Flowers's drawing book which consists of a group of sheets, crudely hand sewn together in the center with drawings of people, several border patterns, birds, and flowers. On this page, the left vase, the scalloped flower on the upper left, and the bell-shaped flower at lower right could be the sources for similar motifs on the right side of Ann's and Mary's coats of arms. *DMMC, WM 87x190, 16. Gift of Mr. and Mrs. Henry Wells.*

her husband's inventory were eight mahogany chairs covered with needle-work and two fire screens, all of which were undoubtedly Mary's work. Three additional tent stitched pictures were listed in the will, making a set of six in the inventory.

While most prosperous married women did little or no embroidery, Mary Alsop continued on at a great rate. In 1774 she dated a larger Queen's stitched pocketbook for herself (plate 22, center bottom). Fine silk knitting in intricate patterns occupied her later works. The names and dates indicate that she made these for her children and grandchildren. She seemed aware of how unusual this later work was because on most of these pieces she also listed her own age.

Another unusual act by Mary Alsop was to hire Ralph Earl to paint

Figure 54. A brown, twill-woven woolen blanket with strong designs in heavyweight crewel yarns in shades of beige, tan, blue, green, and red. The large-scale stitches are flat, herringbone, whip stitch, and French knots. New England; 1800–1835. H. 78"; W. 97".

a portrait of her mother and one of herself in 1792, when she was 52. These are now owned by the National Museum of American Art. Mary died in 1829 at the age of 89.

Strictly speaking, canvas work was a form of crewel embroidery—that is, crewel yarns were used for working on a backing made of linen or silk canvas. However, the term crewel embroidery (see Glossary) usually refers to needlework done with crewel yarns on grounds, including plain and twill-weave linen, plain-weave wools, and muslins. Here the needle worker was not restricted to covering the entire background, as she was when she worked tent stitch.

To the colonial woman, the term crewel meant two-ply, slackly twisted, worsted yarns. Used not only for canvas and embroidery work but for knitting and tambour work as well, crewel yarns varied from very fine (figure 46), for intricate designs and stitches on delicate backgrounds, to fairly coarse (figure 54), for such heavy grounds as blankets. Most needle women patronized fabric and dry goods dealers, who stocked crewels from England. In the May 6, 1754, *New York Mercury,* one merchant, Roper Dawson, advertised his London "Worsted Crewels in Shades." However, only if the family lived in a large port city or if the husband had business in such cities was a woman likely to have access to a dealer who sold crewels in different weights. In general, the city woman had more needlework materials—a variety of crewels, silks, metallic threads, canvases, and well-drawn patterns—from which to choose than did her small-town counterpart. Women in outlying areas may have spun their own yarn to fit their needs.

Although no pieces of American crewel work survive that can be identified as having been worked before the eighteenth century, we do have evidence in the form of inventories that during the seventeenth century American women were doing crewel embroidery to adorn their homes. These inventories reveal that people owned not only crewel yarns but also several varieties of linen and cotton cloth that would have been used as backgrounds for crewel embroidery.

In 1687, Samuel Sewall of Boston ordered needlework supplies from London for his daughters. His letter specified, "white Fustian drawn, enough for Curtins, wallens [valances], counterpaine for a bed, and half a duz. chairs, with four threeded green worsted to work it."[8] The four-ply yarn referred to was a tightly-twisted yarn, thicker than the two-ply common to the monochromatic pieces being worked in England at that time. This reference suggests that the Sewalls were well acquainted with current English embroidery fashions, and they apparently thought well of them. Sewall wanted not only the fashionable crewels but probably matching designs for all the pieces, ready for working. Colonists preferred coordinated interiors and usually decorated an entire room with just one fabric, calling each room by its predominant color. In this case, Sewall was ordering for "the green room"

Surviving early crewelwork and early references show a preference for backgrounds of either fustian or dimity (see Glossary). Dimity differs

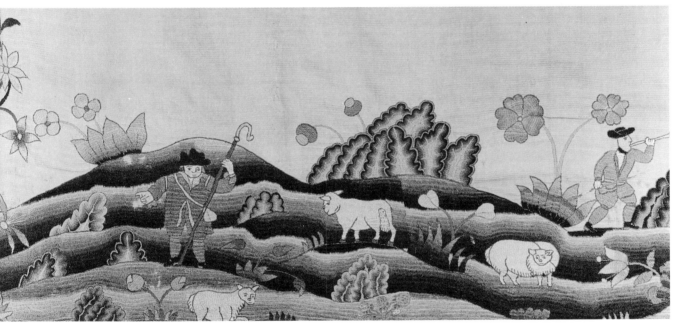

from fustian in that dimity has fine vertical ribs and tufts resembling today's finest corduroy (Figures 55 and 56).

While a woman could order patterns from England as the Sewalls did, she usually prevailed upon someone local to do the designs for her. Occasionally it was a friend or relative known for his or her artistic abilities. Sarah Emery mentioned that her Aunt Sarah "drew a lively vine of roses and leaves" for her skirt (plate 23).[9] Lacking such local amateur talent, the embroiderer could turn to a professional. Those who advertised skill at embroidery designing often plied other occupations, as diverse as portrait painter, engraver, tailor, chaise and harness maker, and, of course, art and needlework teacher.

Today groups of designs can be identified as originating from certain areas, towns, schools, and even from specific artists or teachers. Few were as prolific as the Philadelphia artist Samuel Folwell (plate 31). Not able to consistently receive enough commissions, he traveled as far south as Charleston, South Carolina, for work. Later, he taught drawing in his wife's Philadelphia needlework school as well as drew needlework patterns for the students. Samuel's work and that of his son Godfrey (figures 113 and 114), who took over after his father's death, have some distinctive characteristics. The father often drew graceful, classically clad women with an abundance of lovely soft curls falling around their shoulders. Their bare arms are usually white with flipper-like hands. Godfrey's work is similar, but coarser and less skilled.[10]

When it came to filling in the design, for the most part a young woman chose her own stitches. Unfinished pieces on which the inked drawings are still visible show not only a design outline, but occasionally marks that are suggestive of a stitch, such as dots for French knots or seed stitches (plate 23). By determining herself whether a particular area would be made light and open with spaced seed stitches, have the prickly edge of the buttonhole stitch, or be a strong, positive area worked in a solid stitch like flat stitch, a woman could turn someone else's design into her own unique needlework creation. The choice of colors to be used was also the embroiderer's province, and color shading was taught to girls in needlework classes.

When looking at the needlework pieces, it is important to remember that at this time creativity meant something quite different from what it means today. Artists were expected to adhere to rather strictly defined forms, in which they demonstrated their proficiency first, and only secondly their originality. They often used copy work to perfect their techniques; even the finest American artists copied poses and background features from European prints. A needle worker merited less praise for producing an inferior original design than for tracing or copying a superior one. Her

Plate 16. A vigorous design made for an unusually small easy chair. All of the pieces of this upholstery, including some of the original tapes, were purchased by Henry Francis du Pont years ago without the chair. Said to have belonged to an early Boston family, the upholstery was stitched in cross stitch over two threads of the canvas background. Undoubtedly pre–1750 by its high style design, this example is similar to a few English designs, some of which were advertised here and others drawn here by teachers recently from England. Winterthur conservators made an appropriately styled chair to fit these pieces and, in 1993, upholstered them to resemble original methods.

Plate 17 (following). A beautifully preserved Irish-stitched pocketbook with white basting thread stitched on the flap carries a written history. Started by a young woman, probably in the 1760s, it was left unfinished until 1817 when this same woman, who was then 73, remembered it. She quickly finished the purse (the part inside the basting) and presented it to her granddaughter, Elizabeth Titus Hicks, who recorded the circumstances of her gift. *Mr. Anthony Saunder Morris, a grandson of Elizabeth Hicks, gave this pocketbook to the Chester County Historical Society.*

Plate 18. In general, smaller pocketbooks were made for women. These four Irish-stitched examples in crewel yarns on canvas show the designs most often seen. At left is a "single" pocketbook, displaying zigzag pattern, signed "H W 1760" for a member of the Way family of Chester County, Pennsylvania. H. 3 3/4"; W. 5 3/4". *Gift of Miss Mary Swartzlander.*

At top is a flame design with the name Nathaniel Green. A microscopic examination reveals pattern guidelines for only a small center area. America; 1740–1790. H. 6"; W. 8 1/4".

At right is a diamond-within-diamond pattern by Elinor Brown, dated 1753. Probably Delaware. H. 3 7/8"; W. 5 3/4". *Gift of Mrs. Melva B. Guthrie.*

At the bottom is an unsigned double pocketbook in a carnation-like design. America; 1740–1790. H. 3 7/8"; W. 7 1/8".

Plate 1 The inscription of this canvas work reads, "MARY OOTHOUT HER TABLE CLOATH SEPTEMBER THE * 9 * 1759." Pewter and delftware would have been fashionable tea items when this cloth first graced Mary's tea table. The double cross stitch was used in the center area and for the lettering. Two of the carnations in the vase are worked in cross stitch, the rest of the cloth in Irish stitch. H. 29 1/8"; W. 51 3/4".

creativity was apparently considered best used in interpreting the design with the stitches and colors that displayed her craftsmanship (plates 24 and 25; figure 57).

While any girl or woman could purchase an attractive pattern, skilled instruction, and proper materials, not every woman could produce a pleasing product. Unfortunately for them, a minority of women found needlework distasteful and yet unavoidable in a female's social role. However, the pieces that exhibit a special exuberance and originality signify that some embroiderers must have known great joy in their work (plate 26).

The society that prized beautiful material possessions quite naturally demanded fine craftsmanship. Although colonial artisans were spared the rigid guild system still functioning in Europe at this time, long training and practice were still required of them. Apprenticeship periods of five to seven years produced skilled, meticulously trained craftsmen. Seen in this context, the many years a girl spent mastering the intricacies of fancy sewing, often at the expense of any intellectual training, represented not a failure to appreciate her intellectual possibilities but an investment in her artistic talents. Though this age was hardly free of cultural snobbery, there was a minimum of pretension. People who had little or no education took pride in the fine work they did with their hands because society valued their contributions. It was an age for the appreciation of fine workmanship and its unaffected display.

Sometimes, the display of fine work took precedence over thoroughness. For example, cabinetmakers who customarily lavished great attention and care on the front and sides of a fine piece of furniture saw nothing wrong with ignoring the parts that did not show. They did not stain or sand the backs of pieces or the bottoms of drawers, but only planed those surfaces and sometimes left them rough enough to produce splinters. Similarly, the most exquisitely done needlework surfaces often give no hint of the clumsy knots and long, untidy stitches on the back. Not until the Victorian Age and its fastidious concern for appearances would this sort of needlework be considered unaccomplished. Then, even the back was expected to be neat.

Figure 57. One of a pair, still in bright colors, of a side panel graced by undulating flower vines with five fanciful birds flitting through them. The Shelburne Museum in Shelburne, Vermont, owns a piece with a very similar design. The stitches are flat, whip, back, satin, buttonhole, bullion, weaving, and herringbone. Probably Connecticut; 1750–1785. H. 70 1/2"; W. 33".

The demand for fine embroidery and the esteem such work commanded were so great that a few professional male embroiderers established themselves in the larger colonial cities. Although some of these men called themselves tailors and used their embroidery skills to work fancy buttonholes and trim for both men and women, others plainly identified themselves as embroiderers. In England and parts of the Continent most professional embroiderers were male. They were well known, respected, and organized into guilds. However, guilds were illegal in America. Levy Simons, who advertised periodically in New York City for at least twenty-three years, had probably once been a member of the still-active English Company of Embroiderers, incorporated by Queen Elizabeth in 1561. He continued to refer to himself as an "Embroider from LONDON," even after he had become well established in the colonies. In the *New York Mercury* of October 9, 1758, he gave some indication of the diverse skills of an accomplished professional embroiderer. He advertised that he worked "in Gold or Silver, shading in Silk or Worsted work'd Robins, Facings, Handkerchiefs, Aprons or Shoes, Dresden Work of all sorts, done in the neatest and newest Fashion." In addition, Simons removed spots from and cleaned silk, drew patterns, and by 1777 had added tambour work to his repertoire.

The use of stitches in American crewel work varied from that of English pieces. An example of fine English crewel work often contained twenty or more different stitches, probably because of the influence of the Embroiderers Guild with its rigid standards. American work usually used only four to seven stitches, even for large pieces; solidly embroidered areas were usually worked in a stitch known today as Roumanian couching, Oriental stitch, New England laid, or crewel stitch (figure 58). Contemporary evidence suggests that the colonial term was the flat stitch (see Glossary). We do know that flat stitch occurred far more frequently in American work than in English work. English women preferred to work solidly embroidered areas in the satin stitch or the long and short stitch.

Certain regional preferences show up in crewel work. Large projects such as bed hangings were rarely attempted south of New York. In Pennsylvania women chose to do small items, such as pictures (plate 27) and pot holders, or "Tea Kittle Holders," as Elizabeth Drinker called them (figure 59).

Figure 58. Early American valances were usually unlined, as is this one, worked in four shades of blue crewel. Notice the needlework border imitates expensive tape. Note, too, how solidly the flat stitch appears on the surface and its sparseness underneath. The standard disregard for neatness on the reverse side is clearly visible. Other stitches are buttonhole, whip, herringbone, and cross. New England; 1730–1770. H. 10"; W. 71 1/2".

From New England come many charming petticoat borders (plates 23 and 28), a few needlework pictures (usually similar to the canvas-worked ones), and slip seat covers. Women's pockets, usually worn in pairs, were attached to a tape that was tied around the waist, so that there was a pocket on each hip (figure 60). Even when these pockets were worn under the outer skirt, they were often ornamented in crewel or canvas work. Fortunately, fashion approved of the bulky profile that resulted from a woman carrying

Figure 59. A prim little basket of flowers in polychrome crewels sits in the center of this pot holder's wavy borders. Decorated eighteenth-century pot holders like this one are very thin, usually without interlining, and probably meant for show rather than protection. Stitches are whip, cross, satin, and weaving. Dated 1773 by M W, America. H. 6 1/2"; W. 6 3/4".

Figure 60 (opposite). Crewel-embroidered pair of pockets dated 1777 by M M. Eighteenth-century American pockets tend to be larger than their English counterparts. Stitches are satin, whip, bullion, buttonhole, and French knots. America. H. 18 1/2"; W. 12 3/8".

Figure 61 (left). Three crewel work valances. The top one, with its central cherry tree, is shaped as it was originally cut and has a tiny rolled hem on the edges. It features an unusual color scheme for crewel work: orange-red, brown, yellows, greens, gray, and beiges. Stitches used are in herringbone, satin, whip, and cross. New England; 1725–1775. H. 8 3/4"; W. 56 1/2".

The center valance, worked in two shades of blue, has few solid areas and many rows of herringbone and buttonhole to the outside. This gives the work a characteristic prickly look. Other stitches, seed and French knots. 1750–1800. H. 13 1/2"; W. 67".

The polychrome bottom panel, restyled in form, displays very delicate stitching with fine crewel yarns. New England; 1730–1780. H. 8"; W. 58 5/8".

things like her sewing, keys, and even her pocketbook in these colonial pockets.

The English influence is most apparent in the American crewel work done in the Boston area, with its more precise and formal stitchery and use of delicate, well-proportioned flowers. No doubt much of the Bostonian crewel work was done under the supervision or influence of teachers famil-

Figure 62. Three valances and a head cloth done by one embroiderer. Bright crewel yarns in shades of red, blue, yellow, and green are worked in flat, bullion, buttonhole, chain, seed, whip, and darning stitches. Initials D A T [?] in brown silk cross stitch on the head cloth. The printed tape on the edges is a modern addition. Connecticut; 1740–1780. Valances: H. 11 1/4"; W. 56"; H. 11 1/4"; W. 79 1/2". Head cloth: H. 63 1/8"; W. 63 1/8".

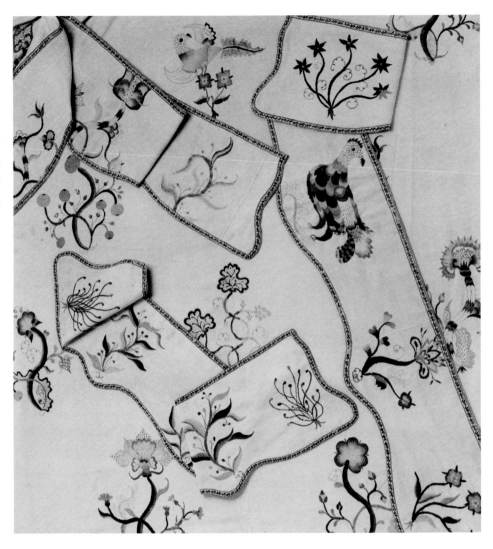

iar with English Queen Anne crewel work.

In the more isolated areas of the colonies, indigenous styles developed. Women in Deerfield, Massachusetts, for instance, produced many pieces in monochromatic blues (probably dyed by the needleworkers themselves). These Deerfield pieces have a characteristically prickly appearance resulting from many of the edgings having been done in the buttonhole stitch. In general, they show a preference for rather open designs with few solidly embroidered areas (figure 61).

The only known crewel work dresses originated in Connecticut. Connecticut crewel work, similar to the region's furniture, was freely designed, flamboyant, and innovative (figure 62). Large, exotic flowers, often topping stems so wide that they needed an inner band of design (plate 29), were often used. Toward the end of the crewel work era, crewel embroidered pieces from the Connecticut River Valley included a number of woolen blankets in vibrant crewel yarns (figure 54). The large-scale, bold designs that they bore were usually worked in proportionately heavier crewel yarns.

Of all the items ornamented with crewel work embroidery, bed hangings presented the most dramatic display—and challenge. Until almost the mid-eighteenth century, many families, regardless of size, lived in houses of only three to five rooms. These rooms had to serve several purposes, and the master bed frequently found itself in the parlor. Since the parlor was also the "company" room, where family visits and teas were held, it was incumbent upon a woman to make these massive pieces of furniture as attractive as possible. Only a woman with great diligence, willing to invest several years of stitchery, would launch such a project, a project calling for the preparation of countless yards of fabric and hanks of yarn before the embroidery could even be started. Later, when the master bedroom was separated from the parlor, the bed retained its importance, as did bed hangings.

A well-appointed bed consisted of three valances (a fourth valance was not essential when the head of the bed stood against the wall, since the head cloth covered that upper area), the head cloth, two narrow side curtains near the head and two large side curtains, each wrapping around either side of the foot posts, a bedspread or coverlet, and bases attached to the bed rail. The lower edge and ends of the valances were shaped in various ways, according to the prevailing style of the day (plates 25 and 29; figure 62). Valances were usually unlined (figure 55), finished only with a fine rolled hem or occasionally edged with tape, and nailed to the framework of the bed.

Some families would hire an upholsterer to fit the master bed with hangings. Made of fine fabrics, they were usually trimmed with an elaborate tape or fringe. The fact that few of these survive today attests to the value a family placed on its homemade work over work done for it by professionals.

Even though bed hangings added to the impressiveness of a master bed, their function first and foremost was to keep the occupants warm. Only the very elderly or the wealthy afforded themselves the luxury of having a fire through the night, and since fireplaces lacked dampers, drafts whipped down into the room when no fire burned. In winter, the temperature inside a home could sink so low that "China cups cracked on the tea table . . . the instant the hot tea touched them," as Sarah Emery noted.[11] In very cold climates, eighteenth-century beds often bore heavy coverings called rugs, which consisted of a sturdy background fabric, such as a heavy linen or woolen blanket, densely set with evenly raised loops of yarn (plate 30; figure 63). Woven bed rugs could also be purchased. (Bed rugs should not be confused with hooked rugs, which came later and were used on the floor. During the eighteenth century, floor coverings were called carpets.)

As the styles in bed furniture changed and hangings lost their popularity, the individual pieces of crewel work were often used for other purposes. Few complete sets of hangings exist today, but the number of individual pieces extant attest to their popularity.

There were numerous other bed linens for the mistress of a household to decorate. While pregnant, a woman would prepare her best sheets, which would be on display when relatives and friends came to visit her as a new mother. The cradle or basket linens were also of import, being carefully marked and perhaps trimmed with lace. Fine crib or christening blankets were made ready, both to keep an infant warm and for show. In New England, new mothers often demonstrated their skills by embroidering a wool blanket with crewel yarns. An 1840 needlework book adopted from *The Spectator*—an early eighteenth-century English magazine popular in the colonies—the rigid stricture that "no one be actually married until she hath the child-bed pillow, &c., ready stitched, as likewise the mantle for the boy quite finished."[12]

This mantle was the baby's christening gown, which was often used

Figure 63. The initials W/R B and the date 1783 on this bed rug are enclosed in a tombstone-shaped frame. The foundation was a mended and patched old woolen blanket, worked in heavy wool yarn in the running stitch. The rhythmic design is worked in shades of blue, white, and dark brown. Probably Norwalk-New London area of Connecticut. H. 90"; W. 87".

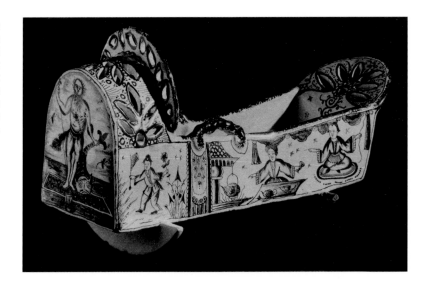

Figure 64. A blue and white delftware cradle used in some areas as a container for small gifts such as pins or money for a new mother during her sitting-up visits. Dated 1736; initialed H T; decorated in Chinese taste; probably Holland.

for generations and sometimes became a family heirloom. In 1758, the inventory of John Turner of Sturbridge, Massachusetts, listed "To fine Little Baby things—10 shillings," probably a reference to the family's christening clothes. Sarah Emery recalled a more common fate for a christening gown: "Grandmother Little owned a famously embroidered, linen cambric christening frock, and this garment having done service at all baptisms was now remodeled for my Sunday dress."[13]

Typical gifts for a newborn and the new mother included a silver coral and bells, a silver spoon, or a pincushion stuck with handmade pins in a pattern (figures 64, 65, 66, 67, and 68). In some regions a pincushion hung on the front door to announce the birth (figure 69).

Busy young mothers could practice their fancy needlework skills only in their spare moments, usually while supervising their bustling households. As a woman sat sewing, she could observe and direct both servants and children and still be productive herself. In this respect, fancy sewing served the same function for a woman of means as plain sewing did for the common housewife; it allowed her time to relax a little.

Relaxation was indeed at a premium in these days, not only in terms of time but also because of the corsets and stays that women "of the better sort" wore. Throughout most of the eighteenth century, corsets rigidly

Figure 65 (top). A *Taufschein*, the baptismal certificate of a Pennsylvania German child. This one marks the birth on December 15, 1827, of Johannes Machemer, son of Jacob and Catharina Machemer of Turbot Township, Pennsylvania.

Figure 66 (bottom). Delftware caudle or posset pot decorated in blue, orange-red, green, and yellow. Caudle was so commonly served at christening parties and visits to the new mother that Webster's 1806 *Compendious Dictionary* called it "child-bed food." Family recipes varied, but the basics included oatmeal, water, lemon, wine, and spices such as nutmeg and mace. Dated 1709, probably Lambeth, England.

127

Figure 67 (top). Traditional gifts for babies were pincushions and rattles. It was thought that coral had health-giving properties. Thus, it was appropriate for teething; the bells and whistle were to amuse. 1740–1760. L. 5 1/2" Rectangular pincushion features a flower design and one word on each side, all formed by tiny pins. They spell, "Welcome / Little / Stranger / Here." The date, 1795, is on the back. L. 7 1/2"; W. 5". S-shaped cushion also says "Welcome / Little / Stranger" on one side; "Love joins / RG. SKG. 1816" is on the back. L. 7 1/2". *Author's collection.*

Figure 68 (bottom). Moveable wooden toy—two pecking roosters. United States or Europe; 1800–1860.

molded the body into an inverted long cone-like form by pushing the bust line unnaturally high and molding the waistline very low. The central placket of the corset usually contained a removable stay called a busk, made of wood or ivory. The rigidity of the stays and busk left the wearer no choice but to practice the erect posture she had been taught in the day and boarding school (figure 70). Only when she was ill or pregnant would a woman appear without the restricting garments. A tutor on the Carter plantation in Virginia, Philip Fithian found it so unusual when Mrs. Carter removed her stays one day that he recorded it in his diary.[14]

Unlike plain sewing, fancywork could not be done at night, since neither candles nor firelight produced sufficient light for this intricate stitchery. Even under the best conditions, the resulting strain on the eyes usually forced a woman to give up fancy sewing by age forty-five or fifty.

A woman was likely to be most productive as a needle worker in the few years between the time she left school and the time she married. During this period, free of responsibilities of running her own household, she had the time to make not only bed linens, towels, and other items for her dowry, but also accessory pieces, many for gifts (figures 71, 72, 73, and 74).

A woman did not stop learning when she left her last sewing class as a schoolgirl. She could pick up a new stitch or the technique for a new effect from the women in whose company she sewed. Or if she lived in one of the bigger cities, she could attend a class to keep abreast of the latest styles. In her January 27, 1774, advertisement in *Rivington's New York Gazeteer*, Sarah Long of London mentioned the subjects she offered to teach young ladies and then added, "GROWN LADIES may be taught the TAMBOUR by lesson, as a room is set apart for that purpose. A compleat assortment of the very best Tambour silks for shadings are provided, with the best needles and cases and will be sold at the lowest prices." Obviously, sewing teachers offered in their advertisements an enticing array of needlework supplies, not just for their young pupils but also for the girls' mothers.

The prosperous women who lived in the prominent cities of Philadelphia, Boston, New York, and Charleston usually had the most time to pursue fancy needlework. Affluent enough to rely on the products and services of bakers, brewers, candle makers, soap makers, fabric merchants, launderers, ironers, dry cleaners, and dressmakers, they had far less of a burden in caring for their homes and families. Moreover, they had their pick of indentured servants and slaves, who were more plentiful in these large port cities. In contrast, women of the better sort in smaller towns, such as Newburyport, Annapolis, Deerfield, Saybrook, and Charlotte, had fewer conveniences and on the whole less time for fancy needlework.

Figure 69. A satin pincushion hung on doors in the New York region to announce the birth of a baby. Handmade pins spell out a revealing eighteenth-century phrase that suggests the distance parents maintained from their newborn children: "Welcome Little Stranger." America, dated 1770.

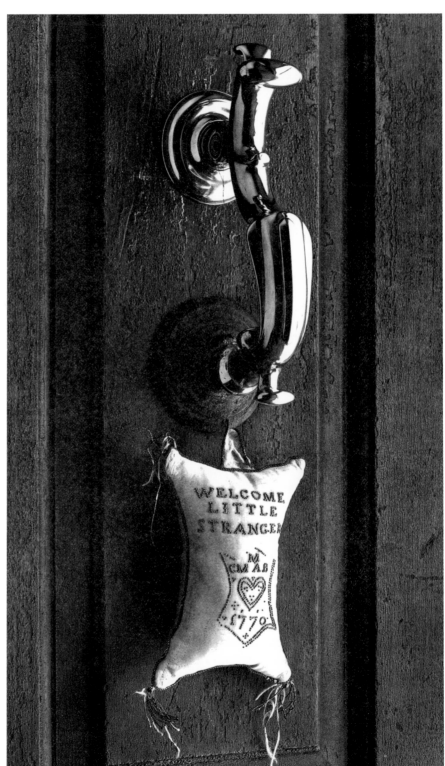

130

Figure 70. Two corsets with multiple stays and two busks lying on a one-piece, light blue silk quilted petticoat. These eighteenth-century corsets forced the body into a long cone-shape and were quite different from the shorter, pinched waist versions adopted in the 1830s. America; 1750–1785.

THE MAJORITY OF these women, wherever they lived, functioned within the confines of their culture. It is important to understand the basic principles of their subordination, in order to appreciate the character of these women and the character they brought to their work. Legally they were the wards of their husbands. Any property or money a woman might have owned before her marriage or any that she earned during it automatically became her husband's sole possession to manage or dispose of as he pleased. Only rarely did a father have the will and foresight to arrange for his daughter a prenuptial agreement that mitigated these rigid laws. Men "exercise nearly a perpetual guardianship over them [women], both in their virgin and their married state; and she who, having laid a husband in the grave, enjoys an independent fortune, is almost the only woman who among us can be called free." So wrote Englishman William Alexander in 1796 in his two-volume *The History of Women,* one of the earliest works on the subject.[15]

Not only did a married woman have no legal rights to her children, but by custom the husband reigned as the final authority in the home. Alexander wrote, "A father only is empowered to exercise a rightful authority over his children, and no power is conferred on the mother."[16] If her husband died, a woman could not expect to gain control of her children automatically. Another man was often appointed their guardian.

As late as 1848, the first Women's Rights Convention, held in Seneca Falls, New York, employed the classic term "civilly dead" to describe a married woman's legal position.[17] And if women were civilly dead inside the home, they were civil nonentities outside. Only men voted, and only they made laws and ordinances, including those that directly affected women. Women were excluded from the political arena, along with the many men who did not meet the restrictive voting requirements of early American society.

This legal subordination of women persisted until the twentieth century. Yet real situations occasionally diverged from legal formality. New England was a rapidly expanding culture of men set on improving their lot, and women proved to be rather handy, indeed necessary, accomplices. Men frequently ignored the legal niceties of keeping women in their places, especially in a place like Nantucket where the seafaring men depended upon their wives to run the home and often a small business while they were gone. Later, this unstructured pioneer atmosphere gave way to a more stuffy propriety when economic growth entailed more sophisticated business arrangements than those of husbands and wives working side by side, as spouses often did in earlier colonial times.

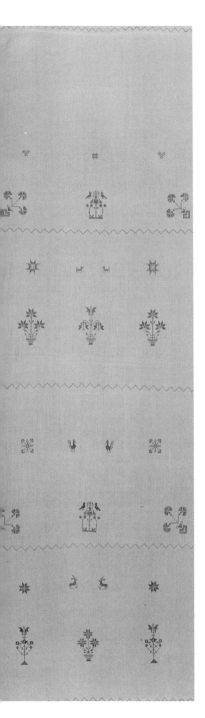

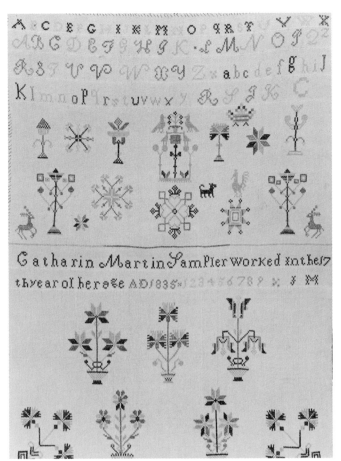

Figure 71 (above). This Lancaster county sampler was more carefully planned than most. Extra threads in two areas were deliberately woven in horizontally as guides for the alphabets, name, date, and legend. Rows of Germanic designs follow the lettered sections in the upper and lower parts. In the middle is "Catharin Martin SamPler Worked in the 17 / th year of her age AD 1835," the numbers 1–9, and initials J M. Pennsylvania samplers were practice pieces for the more important hand towel. Usually not framed, these stayed in a chest and the hand towel was the show piece. H. 18"; W. 13".

Figure 72 (left). A year later, in 1836, Catharin Martin finished her hand towel with all-pink designs carefully arranged. She copied each design from one on her sampler. Never intended for use, hand towels hung on a door to display a girl's ability in the same way that samplers did in English-speaking communities. *Partial funding provided by Vera L. M. H. Goldman.*

Only toward the end of the eighteenth century did women lose access to their husbands' business affairs and experience the tightening of legal restrictions. Throughout the colonial years, however, many spouses had maintained a kind of practical equality in their marriages. Courts went so far as to favor the women who sued to act as their own agents after their husbands had deserted or otherwise shown themselves unable to support them. Because the members of colonial society viewed poverty as sinful, they preferred women who were financially independent, especially if the alternative was for them and their children to become public charges. However, since indigence was considered to be a grave social wrong, a girl's parents usually took care to entrust her only to a husband who had firmly established himself vocationally, thereby demonstrating that he could support a family.

We know that many women assisted their husbands vocationally, since many continued the family business after the man of the house died. To do this successfully, a woman needed to be thoroughly familiar with her husband's trade, for she had to oversee an apprentice or hired journeyman who took over the actual work. Some women carried on by themselves, though not always without encountering resistance. Mary Roberts, the widow of a painter and engraver in Charleston, announced in the *South Carolina Gazette* of February 2–9, 1740, "Face Painting well performed by the said Mrs. Roberts." Apparently, the predominantly male clientele who had patronized her husband needed further persuasion, and on September 12, 1743, she advertised, "It has been reported that the Subscriber cannot print Copies off Copper Plates &c. . . . this is to certify that the same is a manifest Falsehood, for that she is ready and willing to serve all Gentlemen and others as shall be pleased to employ her for that Purpose."

The clever, genteel Mrs. Samuel Provoost of New York became one of the most successful of these widows-turned-entrepreneurs. In order to attract customers to her counting house, located on a side street, she hit upon the idea of installing a sidewalk of flat stones in front of the shop and adjacent to it, along the street. Accustomed to rounded cobblestone or dirt streets, the pedestrians in the city greeted this innovation as a relief as well as a novelty, and Mrs. Provoost gained more business as well as the distinc-

Figure 73 (opposite). An unknown woman, initials M K, created fantastic birds and animals in red and navy cross stitches on this hand towel. The lower section is finished with knotting in a diamond pattern. Pennsylvania; 1800–1870. H. 48 1/2"; W. 13 1/16".

Figure 74. A hand towel by Elisaeet Rauch. In the upper section, flower trees were worked in red and beige cross stitches. The lower square is a coarse panel of drawn work with stars and an angular plant embroidered in white cotton yarn. Pennsylvania; 1800–1850. H. 64 3/4"; W. 16 1/16"

tion of bringing the sidewalk to New York. She was so successful, both socially and financially, that the area of her shop became known as Petticoat Lane. When she remarried in 1721, she took in the business of her husband, enlarging the counting house to include space for his law practice. At the same time, she made elaborate legal arrangements permitting her to carry on her business and to ensure her financial independence. This remarkably successful career woman was also the mother of three children.[18]

Though always a minority, skilled business and professional women—single, married, and widowed—entered a wide range of fields: tavern keeping, paper hanging, dry goods and seed merchandising, upholstering, glass engraving, artistry in wax and miniatures, publishing, importing, midwifery and medicine, laundering, dentistry, brewing, and even circus performing. Most frequently of all, working women earned their living at teaching and needlework, and often both.

Even if they were not needleworkers, the women who participated in fields outside of homemaking give us some insight into the lives of those who were. They show us that, while in the minority, some woman of standing combined the roles of housewife, mother, and professional. They, like their poorer counterparts, did what needed doing, whether it was nursing a sick child or running the family business when the man of the house could not. Working outside the home did not relieve women of their regular household duties. It only added to them, leaving less opportunity or inclination for fancy diversions.

PERHAPS THE MOST demanding form of fancy work that colonial women who had the time produced was lace work, a generic term that includes many delicate open work techniques, all of them requiring great skill and patience. Although the finished product was expensive, and as such a symbol of those wealthy enough to wear it, the task of lace-making hardly pampered those who performed it.

During the years that social custom was dominated by the Puritans, there was social censure for any but those in the higher orders of society

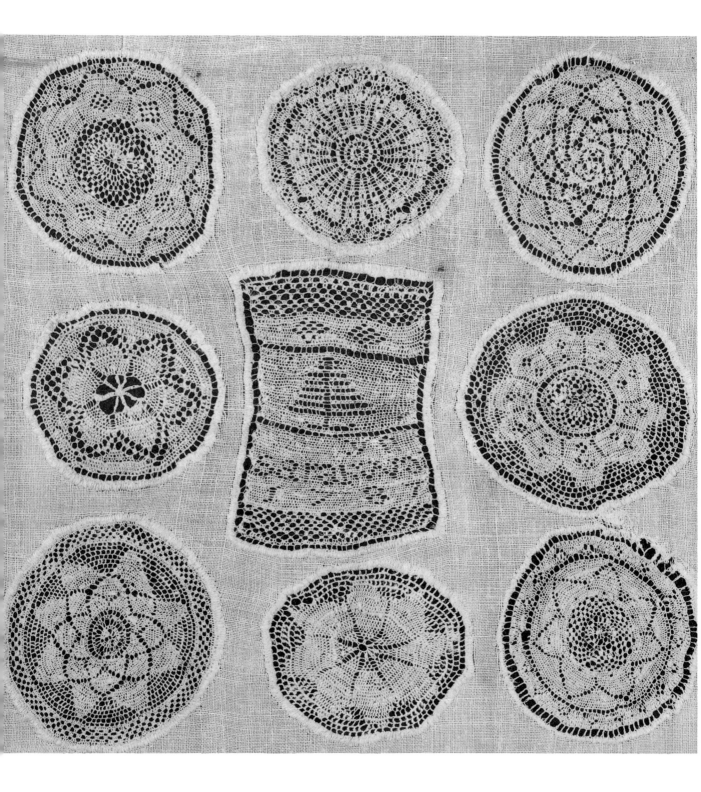

Figure 75 (opposite overleaf) In 1762, Sarah Keen produced her lacy but solidly worked cutwork sampler. This small piece must have taken months of tedious work as she removed the ground fabric section by section and refilled each area with various patterns of detached buttonhole stitches. Pennsylvania. H. 7 1/2"; W. 6".

Figure 76. (overleaf) All-linen cut work, pointing, or needle lace sampler signed by Sarah Wayn[e], 1787. In spite of her proficiency in cutwork, she did not leave enough space to complete her last name. Sarah Wayne was probably the daughter of the Philadelphia cabinetmaker William Wayne. H. 6 7/8"; W. 7 1/8".

Figure 77 (opposite). A particularly graceful example of a combination of cut work, Dresden work, and embroidery. The majority of the examples with a basket of flowers are all white and are earlier than the few pieces like this with separate designs in colored accents. Most of these date from about the mid 1780s to 1795. Here the artistic use of silk shades in blue, gold, and brown add sparkle and life to this unsigned 1795 composition. Philadelphia. H. 11 3/4"; W. 14 1/2".

who wore lace. This behavior prevailed for about as long as it took those a bit lower in the social pecking order to be able to afford lace. During the seventeenth, eighteenth, and early nineteenth centuries, stylish men favored lavish amounts of lace gracing their shirt fronts and cuffs. Women used it to ornament dresses, aprons, handkerchiefs, and baby clothing. By the eighteenth century, the colonies imported sizable quantities of lace from England. In mid-century the better American sewing schools were teaching their girls how to make lace. Advertisements regularly offered all sorts of lace work supplies.

American needleworkers practiced four forms of lace work before the nineteenth century: cut work, Dresden work, netting, and bobbin lace (see Glossary).

The fine white work samplers (figures 75 and 76), products of the day and boarding schools during the last half of the eighteenth century, best illustrate the technique of cut work. Because the work was so fragile, few examples of it remain. To do cutwork, a needle woman embroidered an outline—a square, circle or odd shape—on a linen background with satin or buttonhole stitch. She then cut away the entire enclosed area and filled in the empty space with intricate small-scale patterns of detached knotted buttonhole stitches. This technique was also known as pointing.

In Dresden work, design shapes were outlined in buttonhole, satin, or chain stitches; however, the enclosed areas of fabric were not cut out. Instead, only certain warp and weft threads were removed to create a more open weave fabric. Embroidery stitches were then used to draw the remaining ground threads together into lace-like designs. Usually this drawn thread work was combined with pulled thread work, in which embroidery stitches were used to pull the threads of the ground fabric together to form decorative holes (figure 77). Needlework teachers who advertised instruction in Dresden work sometimes called it weave lace or Berlin needle work (not to be confused with the later, Victorian canvas work called Berlin work). Pennsylvania hand towels (figure 74) often show a coarser form of the drawn work technique.

Bobbin lace—also called bobbin, bobbinet, bone, and pillow lace (see Glossary)—employed a number of slender bobbins of bone or wood, each of

which was wound with thread. By knotting and interlocking the bobbin threads around pins, each inserted vertically into a strategic design point in a pattern laid over a specially made, rounded, firm pillow, the lace maker could create elaborate openwork patterns. Although early in the nineteenth century needlework instructors increasingly advertised bobbinet lace among the skills they taught, it was too complex an undertaking to gain great appeal as an accomplishment. Some women in Ipswich, Massachusetts, earned their living producing bobbin lace in the eighteenth and early in the nineteenth century.

Netting (see Glossary) took its name from the background material used for it—not a plain woven material such as fine muslin, but a fine mesh, either hand made or machine made. The needle worker added embroidery stitches in delicate designs to this net ground. The term net work also indicated the process of creating the background net. By using a variety of different stitches, a woman could produce interesting effects, such as those in the center of the flower shown in figure 78. One of the few advertisements to offer instruction in all lace-like techniques was Elizabeth Wilson's in *The Pennsylvania Ledger and Weekly Advertiser* for May 20, 1775, "Dresden Work, Pointing, Bobbing, and Netting Lace."

Figure 78. Sheer white cotton embroidery partially basted to its inked paper pattern, visible through the fabric (lower left). The flowers were worked in satin stitch with hand made netted centers. Hand made and later machine made net were also used as foundations for lace work. United States; 1790–1810. H. 3 1/2"; W. 4 3/16".

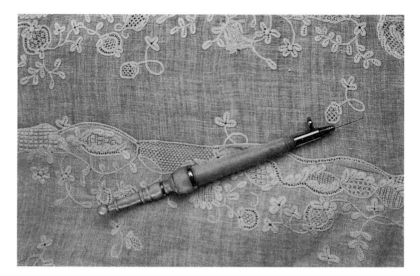

Figure 79. A gold mounted mother of pearl tambour hook lies on a fine cotton collar exquisitely worked in Dresden work, tamboured stems, and buttonholed petals. American, 1790–1825. Photograph by L. Delmar Swan. *Courtesy of Kathleen Epstein.*

Lace work was demanding and time-consuming. Then tambour work (see Glossary) came to America. The first evidence of this new fancy work, which was faster to create than lace, appeared in the late 1760s. A milliner, Mrs. Bontamps, announced in the *Philadelphia Gazette* for December 29, 1768, that she "embroiders in Gold, Silver, Silk and Thread, upon the late invented Tambour." Women without the skill or patience for lace work found to their delight that they could produce a similar effect (figure 79). Using silk, cotton, or fine crewel thread, they employed tambour work to embellish scarves, window hangings, and other accessories. Delicate white-on-white, lacy-looking designs in tambour work were especially popular for the sheer Empire-style dresses.

Instead of a needle, the tambour worker used a hook with a narrow decorative handle and fitted with one from an assortment of various-sized, sharp, V-shaped hooks. Tambour work was done with one hand above and one hand beneath a round frame over which the ground fabric was tautly stretched (plate 10). The tambour worker first inserted the hook down through the stretched fabric, using the hand underneath the frame to loop the thread onto the hook from below. She next pulled the hook and the loop of thread back up through the material, leaving the small loop of thread resting on the material. She then reinserted the hook just inside the first loop to

Figure 80. Tambour-worked fragment in fine colored crewels Probably United States, 1790–1830. H. 8 1/8"; W. 35 1/2". *Gift of Mrs. Francis White.*

bring up a second loop of thread. In this way the tambour worker created a chain of loops, each one anchoring the previous one to the background material (figure 80).

Tambour work established itself rapidly. In January, 1772, for example, one wealthy gentleman from Philadelphia, John Cadwalader, bought a fine wooden tambour frame for his wife, Elizabeth, from the prominent cabinetmaker Thomas Affleck for the considerable sum of two pounds.[19] During the 1770s, numerous newspaper advertisements appeared from teachers offering instruction in tambour work to adult women as well as their daughters. Merchants advertised their lines of tambour work supplies. One such announcement, from *Rivington's New York Gazeteer* of July 17, 1774, heralded "A compleat assortment of TAMBOUR SHADES on SILK and

144 Chapter 3

SHANEIL, with the best London made Tambour needles, and cases." Various merchants in the colonies also imported finished pieces of tambour work.

The practice of handmade tambour work lasted for some fifty years. Then in 1834, at Paris exhibition a machine was unveiled that, with a single operator, could produce tambour stitches at one hundred and forty times the rate of a woman working by hand. Tambour work died as quickly as it had arisen, and today fine handmade projects are virtually nonexistent.

T AMBOUR WORK'S POPULARITY foreshadowed the beginning of a new era in American needlework, and in the life-styles of fancy needle workers. The number of affluent women in the colonies was growing, and these women gradually grew less isolated in their homes. More gregarious

Figure 81. Specially-made child's toy cup, saucer, tea caddy, teapot, and teapot stand of Chinese export porcelain with overglazed decoration picturing a boy and girl playing. Normal-sized tea caddy has an overglazed shield motif. China; 1800–1810

Figure 82. Child's banister-back chair supports a cloth doll that wears a brown chintz dress with rose and white flowers and a plaid apron. The small crewel-embroidered bag has many worn areas, exposing the brown-inked design. The embroidery is crudely executed (possibly by a young child) in whip, satin, and seed stitches.

Plate 20 (left). A useful item, a wall pocket done in the Irish stitch and dated 1766 by M H. rather than being stitched or lined, the inside and back are made of exposed cardboard. Probably Pennsylvania. H. 10"; W. 8".

Plate 21 (right). Finely worked, Irish-stitched canvas cover for a Bible, done with crewel yarns and white silk to outline the design. A different pattern was used for the spine than the covers. There are forty stitches to the linear inch. Written on one of the pages in the Bible, printed in London in 1685, is "Phobe Guest [?] her Bible given her by her mother ye 15 day of ye 10 month 1691." Another entry indicates that Phobe gave it to her daughter Debbe Morris in 1738. The cover was probably worked by Debbe . Philadelphia area, 1730–1770. *Owned by the Chester County Historical Society.*

Plate 22 (top). It is unusual in the twentieth century to obtain a group of works by one woman. These silk bags, purse, sewing cases, and pocketbooks were all worked by Mary Wright Alsop of Middletown, Connecticut. The pocketbook in Queen's stitch has her name, "Mary Alsop x 1774." The other small Queen's-stitched pocketbook, with pink diamonds, is unmarked. She knitted the other pieces in the early nineteenth century. The existing dates and initials indicate that they were presents to her children and their spouses.

Plate 23 (bottom). An unfinished petticoat border in crewelwork. The inked design indicates the outlines and the areas for seed or darning stitches. A bewildered sheep stands on a hillock among strawberries as big as his head. Stitches are flat, whip, French knots, seed, satin, and darning. Said to be from Litchfield, Connecticut; 1725–1775. H. 7 1/4"; W. 95".

Plate 24 (top). One of the best designed and executed bed covers displaying an exceptionally graceful border. The stitches are flat, herringbone, whip, satin, French knots, darning, and bullion. Embroidered in the center top in pink silk is "A. L. to B. S. / 1774." Probably Massachusetts. H. 108 3/4"; W. 87 1/4".

Plate 25 (bottom). Vigorous design on a crewelwork bedspread from Connecticut, probably by the same embroiderer as the valances in Figure 62. Shown here with other crewel work hangings. Stitches are flat, bullion, buttonhole, seed, whip, herringbone, weaving, and chain. Bedspread 1740–1780. H. 93 1/4"; W. 111 1/2".

149

Plate 26 and Cover (top). Detail of the left end of a lively unfinished crewelwork panel (the cover shows the center and right end). Birds as large as people compete for the ripe cherries and pears while various animals and more birds romp among the flowering vines on the hills. Silk yarn was used for many accents. Stitches are flat, whip, seed, French knots, and satin. This embroidery is attributed to Mary Dodge Burnham of Newburyport, Massachusetts; 1725–1760. H 16 1/4"; W. 61 7/8".

Plate 27 (bottom) Elizabeth Taylor's picture dated 1785 is part of a related group of crewel embroidered pictures from Chester County, Pennsylvania. Generally made in two sizes, this is the small size. Characteristically this school used the satin stitch rather than the flat in solid areas. H. 11 1/2"; W. 9 3/4".

ON THE EDUCATION

be a school to fit us for life, and life be
a school to fit us for eternity; if such, I
repeat it, be the chief work and grand ends
of education, it may then be worth inquir-
ing how far these ends are likely to be
effected by the prevailing system.

Is it not a fundamental error to consider
children as innocent beings, whose little
weaknesses may perhaps want some correction, rather than as beings who bring
into the world a corrupt nature and evil
dispositions, which it should be the great
end of education to rectify? This appears
to be such a foundation-truth, that if
I were asked what quality is most important in an instructor of youth, I should
not hesitate to reply, such a strong impression of the corruption of our nature, as
should insure a disposition to counteract it;
together with such a deep view and thorough
knowledge of the human heart, as should
be necessary for developing and controlling its
most secret and complicated workings. And
let us remember that to know the world,

as

Figure 83. Detail of Hannah More's influential two-volume *Strictures on the Modern System of Female Education* (volume 1, p. 64). In this passage she sounded her disapproval of the long-held belief that children were born corrupt in nature. DMMC, WM, LC1421/M.83.

and sophisticated, they had less time for the most demanding and intricate needlework forms. Tambour work brought them the rewards of fancy needlework without requiring quite so much effort and concentration. In short, fancy needlework, like life in general, was becoming a bit easier.

Interestingly, and naturally enough, as mothers indulged themselves more, they began to indulge their children more (figures 81 and 82). By the late eighteenth century, enlightened advisors on child-rearing began to recommend more lenient discipline for children when they were disobedient.

[W]hen Encouragement will do no good, Correction becomes Seasonable; when all fair Means and Perswasions prevail not, there is a necessity of using sharper; let that be first try'd in words. I mean not by railing and foul Language, but in a sober yet sharp Reproof. And if that fail too, then proceed to Blows. . . . the Power of Parents over their Children . . . should be exercised with Equity and Moderation.[20]

This was quite a departure from the standard procedure of humiliations and whippings as a first resort. Diaries reveal that even such cultured men as William Byrd of Virginia and Samuel Sewall of Massachusetts frequently countenanced such severe punishments in their households.

It took some time for the modified view to gain support, but by 1804, the thoroughly respectable Englishwoman Hannah More was preaching in her *Strictures on the Modern System* that children's "little weakness may perhaps want some correction," but that children are not "beings who bring into the world a corrupt nature and evil disposition" (figure 83).[21] The doctrine of original sin, which had ruled—or at least rationalized—the governing of children (and everyone else) for so long, had begun to lose its power. Soberness was no longer the prevailing theme for one's behavior, and enjoyment was more acceptable for all. Fancy needlework was soon to reflect this more leisurely view.

Plate 28 Fragment of a crewelwork panel, perhaps a petticoat border, with very fine yarns skillfully worked in flat, whip, and seed stitches. H. 25 15/16"; W. 7 7/16".

Plate 29 Winterthur has displayed this handsome bedspread with its unusual strap work pattern for more than forty years. A few years ago the head cloth with strap work, using the identical green and white wool and silk tape, the same crewel yarns, similar flowers, and workmanship, came on the market. Also acquired at that time was a third piece, which has even more elaborate embroidery; unfortunately, its tape was removed in the 1920s. The bed cover has been attributed for many years to Lydia Hancock, John Hancock's adoptive mother (the cock, sitting on a tree stump at lower center symbolized the Hancock family). The two more recent acquisitions descended through a collateral line. Whether John Hancock's wife Dorothy transferred these pieces to collateral descendants or whether the Hancock connection is false is a matter of speculation. 1725–1740. H. 112"; W 78 1/2". Head cloth H. 73 3/4"; W. 61 3/4". (*Karin Bengtson researched the family connections and other known pieces for the above identification.*).

The Golden Years of Needlework 153

Plate 30 Mary Foot[e], who lived in Colchester, Connecticut, created this darned bed rug, presumably for her marriage in 1778 to Nathaniel Otis. Mary started with a plain woven woolen ground and sewed her design in large, blue darning stitches, pulling each stitch level and tautly. She did not leave the raised loops customarily found in bed rugs. The white background is completely covered in an even-textured darning pattern. Mary's sister Elizabeth made a similar rug, now owned by the Connecticut Historical Society. A third one, probably by her sister Abigail, is at Historic Deerfield, Inc. H. 83 1/2"; W. 77 1/2".

154 Chapter 3

NOTES

1. Will of John Morris.
2. Swan, "Worked Pocketbooks," 298-303.
3. Emery, *Reminiscences*, 34.
4. Diary of Elizabeth Drinker, May 9, 1760;. pincushion, January, 1760; tweezer case, July, 1760; Bible cover, before March 9, 1760.
5. Ring, *Girlhood Embroidery*, vol. II, 338.
6. Linda Baumgarten, personal communication, 1993. This piece is owned by Colonial Williamsburg Foundation.
7. Krueger, "Mary Wright Alsop," 25.
8. Sewall. "Letter-Book of Samuel Sewall," 44.
9. Emery, *Reminiscences*, 38.
10. Deutsch, "Collectors' Notes," (128, no. 9): 526–527; (130, no 4): 646–647; (137, no. 3): 616–624.
11. Emery, *Reminiscences*, 312.
12. Countess of Wilton, *Art of Needle-Work*, 354.
13 Inventory of John Turner, Emery, *Reminiscences*, 15.
14. Fithian, *Journal & Letters*, 207.
15. Alexander. *History of Women*, vol. 2, 338.
16. Alexander, *History of Women*, 343.
17. Calhoun, *Social History*, vol .2, 119.
18. Van Rensselaer, *Goede Vrouw*, 234–36, 261–63.
19. Bill from Thomas Affleck to John Cadwalader, January 27, 1772.
20. [Wray], *Ladies Library*, vol. 2, 161.
21. More. *Strictures*, vol. 1., 64.

4 Diversions for Genteel Ladies: The Age of Accomplishments

Figure 84 (opposite). Elizabeth Tunnecliff stitched this almost solidly worked sampler-mourning piece in 1791. While Adam stands idly by, Eve, holding an apple, pets the snake. Above is an imposing building. More important is the urn to the right, with bald wispy branches curved over it. This is currently the earliest known mourning symbol in American needlework. Elizabeth probably went to school in Albany, New York, as several families of Tunnecliffs lived nearby. H. 20 5/8"; W. 16 3/8".

FOR WOMEN WITH sufficient wealth to keep up with evolving styles, the end of the eighteenth century and the beginning of the nineteenth was an exhilarating time. They could—and were expected to—do more than sit home and manage their households. Many new intellectual outlets and possibilities for socializing beckoned. Though much of this new social life was frivolous, serious ideas about the proper role of women were fostered. "In the present state of society," a prominent male Philadelphian wrote in 1810, "woman is inseparably connected with everything that civilizes, refines, and sublimates man."[1]

The observer, Joseph Hopkinson, was writing as a friend of the fine arts, complimenting women for their interest in advancing cultural ideals. But his words might just as easily have served as the rationale for all the other forms of social activity in which women of the better sort participated during this period. In an age in which wealthy Americans strove to be genteel, women were considered the most capable of appreciating, indeed nurturing, gentility.

In 1784 Nancy Shippen Livingston was a twenty-one-year-old woman living with her parents after she had separated from her husband. She was no longer the mistress of a household and what she did with her leisure time resembled more a single girl's pastimes than a married woman's. One of her activities was to record how she thought a lady of her station should spend each day. The schedule she proposed no doubt overemphasized the new priorities of the fancy ladies of the day; nevertheless, her recommendations are intriguing. She allotted two hours a day for household management and five hours for accomplishments such as sewing and drawing—in which she included the instruction and observation of servants as they did household chores. Then she added three hours for meals, heavily laden with conversation, and five more hours for socializing.[2]

Five hours a day of socializing! To fill such a schedule required more than incidental contact with a few friends. Starting in the last quarter of the eighteenth century, urban women of Nancy Shippen Livingston's social class engaged in an elaborate round of visiting and receiving visits. In diaries kept at this time by fashionable ladies, there is hardly a day's entry that does not mention one or two visits.

Some visits were made to acknowledge a special occasion. For example, two or three weeks after a woman had given birth, she entertained her acquaintances at a "sitting up visit," during which callers could admire the good health of the baby and leave presents.

A marriage merited a "bride's visit," in some areas as soon as a day after the ceremony but as long as a month afterward in others. In 1786, Hannah Thomson, wife of a Philadelphia government official, noted that in New York the husband as well as the bride received congratulatory callers: "The Gentlemans Parents keep open house just in the same manner as the Brides Parents. The Gentlemen go from the Bridegroom house to drink Punch with and to give joy to his Father. The Brides Visitors go In the same manner from the Brides to his Mothers to pay their compliments to her."[3]

Such special events as births and marriages occurred too infrequently to satiate the desire for socializing that the newly gregarious ladies of the day possessed. Instead of waiting for special occasions, these women made visiting an integral part of their daily routine. Sarah Emery noted that in her town of Newbury, Massachusetts, "fashionable ladies devoted the morning to calling or receiving visitors. . . . There was little ceremonious visiting of an afternoon, unless invitations had been issued for a tea party" (figure 85).[4] However, in most regions, visiting was customarily done in the afternoon.

At their get-togethers, women might snack on cake and wine or play cards, all the while having some relatively undemanding kind of fancy needlework such as tambour or knitting nearby. Above all, of course, they talked. Since the tempo of an afternoon was bound to lag without it, good conversation became an essential ingredient for a successful visit, whatever the other diversions. When Rebecca Franks, a Philadelphian, visited New York City in 1781, she wrote home to her sister in disgust, "few New York

Figure 85. A Newport pierced gallery tea table set with a group of molded English salt-glazed stoneware. When a silver spoon was laid across a tea cup, it signified the guest wanted no more tea. A pot holder of crewel work on a diaper ground lies handy. Stitches are seed, chain, whip, and flat. Pot holder: New England; 1740–1780. H. 7 5/8"; W. 6 7/8".

ladies know how to entertain company in their houses unless they introduce the card tables . . . I don't know a woman or girl that can chat above half an hour, and that on the form of a cap, the colour of a ribbon or the set of a hoop-stay."[5]

In addition to daytime visiting, there were dinner parties and balls to attend at night. Sarah Emery noted in her reminiscences:

> *Dinner parties were common, when the table would be loaded*
> *with luxuries. After dessert the ladies retired to the parlor for an*
> *hour's gossip, while the gentlemen sipped wine, smoked long*
> *Dutch pipes, and discussed the affairs of the nation. The ladies*
> *having been rejoined in the drawing room, coffee was passed.*

Martha Turner

Litiz Seminary,

JUNE 15, 1837

She recalled that dances were held in a specially-built hall, considered excellent for dancing because it had a spring floor. While the young courting couples danced, their parents played cards in anterooms.[6]

This increased socializing by women did not alter the fact that certain basic aspects of their lives had not changed. The Declaration of Independence, and most of the subsequent enlightened writings, pertained exclusively to the rights of white males. Women's subordinate legal role remained. While historians disagree on the effects of the post-Revolutionary War period on women, there is no denying that it was a transitional period for them. Some historians believe that this era marked the end of an economic partnership between women and their mates, an end that resulted in women's loss of stature. Other historians claim that the expanding economy and the Industrial Revolution offered women not only more leisure time, but at least briefly varying degrees of benefits from the enlightened ideas.[7] Without question, women's scholastic opportunities improved owing to the enlightenment, though the seminaries continued to stress an ever-widening group of accomplishments. Painting on velvet, singing, piano playing, water colors, and hair work vied with the new needlework forms for the fashionable young woman's attention.

In dating the various needlework fads of this period, the extraordinarily well-kept records of the Moravians are most informative since the Moravians taught most of these accomplishments at their school in Bethlehem, Pennsylvania. References to glass beads, for example, begin to appear in the Moravian accounts of the 1790s. To have a "Glass Pocket Book" made up cost "Cath. Boudinot 1 £, 6s, on June 17, 1797." Glass beads were also used to decorate pincushions, needle holders, and bags.

Beginning in 1818, the sisters at the Moravian schools in Bethlehem and Lititz, Pennsylvania, and in Salem, North Carolina, introduced two new techniques rarely practiced elsewhere: ribbon work and crepe work (see Glossary).[8] Ribbon work was a technique in which one gathered and tacked down a narrow ribbon, about one quarter inch wide. This ribbon was specially dyed in graduated shades of one color. Students beautified small items such as the sewing case in figure 38 with this technique. In crepe work strips of silk crepe were cut, folded, and gathered to simulate a bou-

Figure 86 (opposite). A later form of Moravian work where the silk crepe flowers rise about an inch above their silk twill ground. Here the crepe work is combined with embroidered tendrils, some small leaves in chenille yarns, some in ribbon work, and a few embroidered in whip stitches. Signed in the newly fashionable Gothic lettering, "Martha Turner / Lititz Seminary. / June 13, 1837." It is still in its original, wide slanted gold leaf frame with a reverse, painted mat. Needlework only: 18" square.

Figure 87. Many schools taught painting on velvet to young girls during the second quarter of the nineteenth century. Here an early example of the craft was applied to the Hamilton family arms, though coats of arms were unusual subjects for velvet painting. On this example, an 1813 newspaper was glued to its stretcher.

quet or wreath of flowers (figure 86). Such a design could project an inch or more from the background and thus required a deep frame; those without glass were great dust-catchers.

Painting on velvet, yet another accomplishment, enjoyed a vogue in New England and the middle states during the first third of the nineteenth century. The girls and women who did this work favored simple fruit-and-flower scenes or mourning themes (figure 87).

Women did Marseilles quilting (see Glossary) to make their petticoats showy. Because many stylish dresses before 1800 were fashioned with an open panel in front from the waist to the hem, the front of the petticoat was beautifully displayed. Like tambour work, Marseilles quilting was a holdover from the pre-Revolutionary period. Advertisements dated as early as 1749 mentioned this technique.

The term Marseilles quilting was actually a misnomer. By definition quilting binds together three layers of fabric, and in this technique only two are joined, with artistically shaped areas of filling between them. The finished product resembled those done with the techniques known today as stuffed work and corded work. To work a piece of Marseilles quilting, the needle woman picked a loosely woven cotton or linen to use for a backing fabric. Chosen for the front was a satin or fine plain woven fabric whose highlights would be best set off by the contours of the filling to come. She then applied a design to the underside of the backing fabric, outlining the shape of every area to be filled. She next stitched the two fabrics together along the design lines (figure 88), using fine running or back stitches. Finally, she used a sharp instrument to spread apart several threads of the background fabric and insert cotton batting into each outlined area to create padded design areas. To pad flower stems or other narrow channels in the design, she would thread a large-eyed needle or bodkin with candlewick yarn and run it through the back of the work between the parallel lines of stitching (figure 89).

Beginning about 1760, notices appeared advertising imported, machine-made Marseilles quilting, as for example, "Loom quilting for Petticoats" in the *South Carolina Gazette* of May 21, 1772. Elizabeth Drinker mentions purchasing this loomed quilting on May 4, 1778, when she "went out again after dinner to Shops, [and] bought merceals Quilting for Petticoats for the Girls."[9]

Despite industrial competition, women continued to practice handmade Marseilles quilting until the 1830s. After 1800 open-front dresses went out of style. Instead of petticoats, women then used Marseilles quilting to make bed hangings and dressing table covers (figure 90). Obviously dressing table covers were for show; the raised areas did not provide an even surface for bottles. After the 1830s, cheaper, more durable factory made Marseilles spreads replaced the hand made products. These machine made textiles remained popular for so long (well into the twentieth century) that women of more recent times did not realize that Marseilles quilting had once been a hand embroidery technique.

Candlewicking is a modern term for what was called "knotted counterpaine" in the United States and "Bolton" in England and much of Canada

Figure 88. Hand-drawn paper pattern for stuffed work. Grapes and pineapples were favorite motifs because the small segments could be filled and puffed up attractively. DMMC, WM, 75x132.

Figure 89. Detail of stuffed and corded work, called Marseilles work. The left side shows the finer, upper layer of fabric in a raised pomegranate design. The right side illustrates the coarser under-fabric, with heavy yarn corded through the narrow channels to simulate narrow vines. Worked in 1815 by Mary Remington of East Greenwich, Rhode Island.

Plate 31 A mahogany paint box and a page from an album owned by Eleutheria du Pont Smith. Young women often demonstrated their artistic accomplishments by means of watercolors. The Marquis de Lafayette wrote in the front of this book when he visited Wilmington on July 25, 1825. *DMMC, WM, 65x623.1.*

Plate 32 "Calliope and Clio" is one of Samuel Folwell's most extravagant designs; it epitomizes fashionable classicism and is full of symbolism. Clio (the woman painting a likeness of George Washington) is the muse of history. Calliope (the woman reading from a book) is the muse of epic poetry. The prominent building to the right is a watercolor rendering of the then new Pennsylvania Academy of Fine Arts, finished in March, 1806. Folwell published an etching of it similar to this for the frontispiece of the first copy of the *Philadelphia Repertory*, Mary 5, 1810. It was this Academy which praised women's needlework and art entries in an exhibit of 1812. While the picture is attached to its original stretcher and retains its original glass, on the back of the newer frame in modern writing is, "Made by / Sarah Catherine Skinner Ward / at Miss Maltby's School in Philadelphia in 1816 / She was the wife of Naburn Ward / of Marietta Ohio / Picture was carried on horseback / from Philadelphia." Samuel Folwell did sell his designs to other teachers. H. 18 3/8"; W. 25 1/4".

166 Chapter 4

Plate 33. Sarah Wentworth Apthrop Morton (1759–1846) of Boston, in her early forties, painted by Gilbert Stuart. She was a member of Boston's elite society, both by birth and her marriage to Perez Morton. She took full advantage of the few years of women's enlightenment to publish her poetry, articles, and books.

Plate 34. A handsome coat of arms worked mostly in silk yarns with a little crewel tent stitch. An unusually bright, unfaded green ground with solid gold thread embroidered on the crown, visor, and around the crest. Silver stitches fill in behind the heart, part of the visor, the two diagonal squares of the arms, and the lower banner. It portrays the arms of Matthew Cushion of Hingham, Massachusetts. 1750–1760. Needlework, each side 22".

Partial funding provided by Vera L. M. H. Goldman.

Plate 35 A sprightly picture, probably intended as a mourning picture, by Lucy Nye, who noted that she was born April 4, 1799. Lucy apparently had no one to mourn, so instead of a name on the tomb she substituted a cheerful verse on paper: "Blossoms fruit/and flowers/together rise/and the whole/year in gay/confusion lies." Stitches are whip and satin; face and arm are painted. Paper inserts are glued on the tomb and at the bottom. United States; 1810–1820. H. 11 1/4"; W. 10 7/8".

(see Glossary). Like Marseilles quilting, it was both hand and loom made. The earliest known example is the loom woven variety, dated 1773. To do the hand made method the needleworker used a soft, medium weight cotton ground and embroidered it with soft, bulky yarns that resembled candlewicks, hence the modern name of the yarn and the technique (figure 91). Sometimes women limited themselves to one or two stitches, usually French knots and the whip stitch, producing a rather formal pattern. On other pieces, they used many different stitches and changed the thicknesses of the yarns, creating more exuberant designs (figure 92).

A glance at the back of a piece of candlewick quickly reveals whether it was made by machine or by hand. If machine made, it is smooth, neat, and even; if hand made, it is likely to be a messy hodgepodge of knots, loops, and stretched yarns. Machine made candlewick, with traditional designs, remains popular today.

In addition to all these new needlework forms, many fine sewing accessories were produced during this period. Now, in a more affluent society, with its new regard for feminine refinement, women gained their own fine furniture, intended for both practical use and display. Inlaid and veneered wood worktables were among the first pieces of fine furniture made specifically for women. To be sure, women had always had such essential work accessories as spinning wheels, yarn winders, looms, and embroidery frames. But until this time, the selection of fine furniture had been a man's province. Early sewing tables, for example, came with a decorative cloth or wooden bag that served as a holder for needlework supplies (figure 93). This is probably the first furniture form made specifically for women in America.[10] Such a table was assuredly the prized display piece for a hostess welcoming guests to her parlor.

Until the mid-eighteenth century in America, needleworkers had made do with little more than pins, scissors, needles, and thread. After the Revolution, the stylish trappings of the craft were becoming almost as important as the needlework itself. For example, there were beautiful sewing boxes; whalebone yarn winders; enameled, carved ivory, silver, and mother of pearl needle holders; miniature boxes with miniature tools; silver filigree tools; sets of mother-of-pearl tools; chatelaines; and knitting needle holders

Figure 90 (right). Half-oval dressing table cover of fine white cotton; "Peace" is stitched in script letters over a central eagle, flanked by roosters and dogs. The initials MAW are said to be those of a member of the Westervelt family of New York; 1800–1830. H. 23 3/4"; W. 34 1/2".

Figure 91 (opposite). Candlewick bedspread on a huckaback weave, boldly initialed H G. Predominantly French knots with chain, whip, satin, and interwoven running stitches. United States; 1800–1830. H. 98"; W. 98".

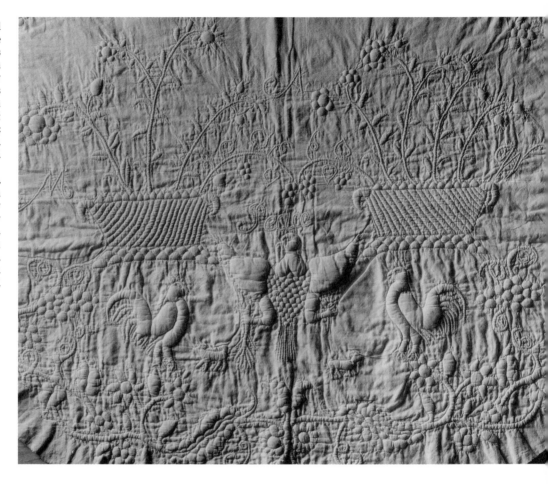

(figures 94, 95, 96, and 97). Until well into the nineteenth century, the vast majority of needlework tools were imported. Thimbles and sailors' work are notable exceptions.

Even with these lovely needlework props and accessories, the early nineteenth century saw a definite decline in the quality of needlework. The pride in meticulous craftsmanship in both women's needlework and many men's crafts began to lose its importance. Apprenticeships for both men and women shortened and finally disappeared. At the same time, young girls spent fewer hours on fancy needlework training. Grown women no longer had the time or patience to create such ambitious, involved projects as canvas work chair seats or upholstery. Now ladies of style preferred fancywork

projects that were less involved and more portable, as well as showier. Needlework continued to have prestige as a feminine accomplishment, though now as a mark of gentility rather than craftsmanship.

A notice in the *Pennsylvania Gazette* for February 17, 1813, announcing the Third Annual Exhibition of the newly formed Pennsylvania Academy of Fine Arts, read, "In the last exhibition there were several productions (the work of female artists) consisting of original drawings, models in wax, pieces of needlework, &c., which were pronounced, by the best judges, equal to anything of the kind executed in Europe" (plate 31).

Women of the previous generation would not have thought of publicly exhibiting their fancy needlework. There had been honor enough in using it to ornament the furnishings of the home. Now, however, fancy needlework acquired a totally new function; it served to display a fashionable lady's genteel sensibilities. In some circles, a woman who did fine needlework ceased to be a craftsman and became an artist. A woman who appreciated such work could consider herself a patron of the arts.

In 1810, after the Pennsylvania Academy's First Annual Exhibition, Joseph Hopkinson rhapsodized in the *Port Folio,* "Our collection of painting and statuary, from the first exhibition, has been visited by our ladies, with a constancy which acquits them of the motive of mere curiosity, and an ardour which could be found only in minds well improved, touched with the fire of genius, and really capable of enjoying her works" (plate 32). For Mr. Hopkinson, "the fire of genius" that sparked a woman to paint, draw, or do fancy needlework went hand in hand with "minds well improved." It was in this context that he remarked that "[women are] inseparably connected with everything that civilizes, refines, and sublimates man." He did not

Figure 92. Exceptionally high tufting on this white candlewick spread by E H in 1827. The mounds were clipped to realistically shape them. Stitches are French knots, satin, and bullion. United States. H. 103"; W. 106".

Figure 93. One of the finest mahogany Boston sewing tables known, possibly by John and/or Thomas Seymour. The veneered figured birch panels are bordered by rosewood. "John Parker, Jr" is stamped underneath the top. By pulling out the bottom drawer one can reach into the work bag. 1800–1810.

Figure 94. A group of sewing tools made of silver filigree: scissors and case; tiny needle case and thimble holder; tape measure; thimble; a low round wax holder; tube-like bodkin holder; scalloped, tube-like etui with a bottom which unscrews for needles and at the other end a scissors, knife, and an engraved bodkin. The oval lidded case hold two tiny cut glass bottles for perfume or alcohol. These were necessary to keep one's fingers clean while working on delicate fabrics. England, 1780–1835. Photograph by L. Delmar Swan. *Author's collection.*

define "everything," but clearly he meant to include women's artistic, intellectual, and aesthetic sensibilities.[11]

As one facet of their personality, women of the better sort during these years were allowed to be lavishly self-indulgent, luxuriating in all the feminine high fashions and diverting entertainments of the day. They wore elegant clothing, played cards, went dancing, attended dinner parties and the theater, witnessed tight-rope performances and equitation acts, and, above all, visited, spending hours each day simply chatting with each other. Many husbands encouraged their wives in this luxurious leisurely life-style, probably because when one's wife had time to spend in this way, it signified a his success.

Yet the idea of gentility required some intellectual as well as social refinement; a fashionable lady could not afford to be ignorant. The same boarding schools that were training their young ladies in the latest stylish accomplishments were also teaching them an expanded range of scholastic subjects. Women attended lectures on philosophy and ethics, visited the new natural history and art museums, wrote poetry, and published articles and books. Some women in a few of the large cities went so far as to hold a very modest form of a salon where men and women discussed the new ideas as well as the new fashions of the day. The Age of Enlightenment was not confined to men, and genteel women as well as men were expected to cultivate their minds.

A few women of the period achieved renown for their worldly activities. Sarah Apthrop Morton, an active Bostonian who sponsored salon groups, published poetry, articles, and books under her pen name "Philenia." With her husband, Perez, she crusaded for repeal of the Boston law banning theater performances (plate 33). In 1791, seventeen years before the government passed a law outlawing the slave trade with Africa, she pleaded for an end to the trade. In the preface to *The Ruling Passion* by Thomas Paine, published in 1797, she was praised as "the American Sappho."[12]

This new style of female sophistication and women's widening horizons were reflected dramatically in contemporary women's fashions. The last decade of the eighteenth century brought to America, as it did to Europe, a vogue for classicism. Roman motifs symbolized the new republican form of government. About 1800, women adopted the classical style in their dress, thereby initiating one of the most radical changes in fashion history. In 1837, *The Young Lady's Friend* reviewed the fashion revolution this way:

> [T]he ladies who had been encased in whalebone, buckram, and [an] abundance of quilted petticoats, stepped forth as Grecian goddesses, without any corsets, any petticoats, any fulness to their garments, or any heels to their shoes. White muslin dresses of the scantiest dimensions [were] drawn closely round the figure, with the shortest possible waists.[13]

After centuries of covering themselves with layer upon layer of clothes and rigid stays, even the most mature women adopted this slim,

Figure 95 (above). A sewing box made in the shape of a piano. The fitted upper tray shows its ivory and mother-of-pearl tools. The miniature piano contains a music box as well. England; 1800–1825.

Figure 96 (right). Swift, or yarn winder, made of whalebone has elaborate urns and acorn finials. Made by Nathaniel Dominy V of East Hampton, Long Island; 1800–1810. *Funds for purchase from the Crestlea Foundation.*

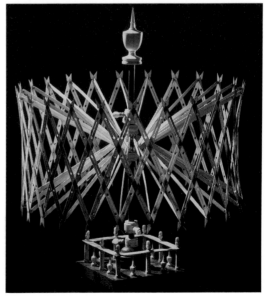

high-waisted silhouette. Such prominent women as Dolley Madison wore this style although their garments were usually made of fabric less-revealing than the younger women dared to wear. A gentleman who attended the wedding of Betsy Patterson and Jerome Bonaparte on Christmas Eve, 1803, remarked, "All the clothes worn by the bride might have been put in my pocket.... Beneath her dress she wore but a single garment." That garment would have been a chemise, a woman's sole concession to underwear and hardly enough to keep the libertines at bay. John Fanning Watson tittered that the clothes were "so thin and transparent ... especially when between the beholder and a declining sun, as to make a modest eye sometimes instinctively avert its gaze."[14]

The conservatives were scandalized, of course. Hannah More gasped at "the unchaste costume, the unpure style of dress, and the indelicate statue-like exhibition of the female figure, [with] its seemingly wet and adhesive drapery."[15] Her description of "wet and adhesive drapery" sounds extreme, but a few women would actually immerse their clothing in water to accentuate the clinging quality of the classical drapery. No doubt those who adopted this racy new costume secretly enjoyed provoking the cries of outrage. Better educated, more sophisticated, and encouraged to express themselves, women were testing their new freedom, often defiantly. A few of them began to take on the previously unassailable topic of male superiority—even in print.

Writing in the September 1787 issue of the *Columbian Magazine*, one woman confessed that she thought women generally could employ their time better than in "scribbling," but she said that she felt compelled nevertheless to "lay down the needle and take up the pen." She wrote in reply to an article in Mathew Carey's *American Museum* that had twitted fastidious women who whitewashed the interior of their homes nearly every spring. (In the days before wire window screens, flies and other insects spotted and disfigured interior walls.) The male writer had noted that the bustle with which women pursued this housekeeping chore inevitably produced a wreckage of "halves of China bowls, cracked tumblers, broken wine glasses, tops of tea pots and stoppers of departed decanters." In refutation, this woman recounted the following experience with her husband:

> *He comes into the parlour the other day, where, to be sure, I was cutting up a piece of linen. Lord, says he, what a clutter here is—I can't bear to see the parlour look like a taylor's shop—beside I am going to make some important philosophical experiments ... You*

> *must know my husband is of your wou'd be philosophers—well,*
> *I bundled up my linen as quickly as I could, and began to darn a*
> *pair of ruffles; which took up no room and could give no of-*
> *fence—I tho't however, I would watch my lord and master's im-*
> *portant business.*

As it turned out, the "philosophical experiments" had a devastating effect on the parlour-turned-laboratory. The woman described the mess, and then continued archly,

> *[T]ell your friend the white-wash scribbler, that this is one means*
> *by which our closets become furnished with 'halves of China*
> *bowls, cracked tumblers, broken wine glasses, tops of tea-pots and*
> *stoppers of departed decanters.' . . . I said nothing, or next to*
> *nothing; for I only observ'd very pleasantly . . . why philosophers*
> *are called literary men is because they make a great litter. . . .*
> *I was certainly the best philosopher of the two: for my experi-*
> *ments succeeded [that is, after she cleaned up after him] and his*
> *did not. . . . My carpet, which had suffered in the cause of ex-*
> *perimental philosophy in the morning, was destined to be most*
> *shamefully dishonoured in the afternoon, by a deluge of nasty to-*
> *bacco juice—Gentlemen smoakers love segars better than carpets.*

The story (and the tirade) ended with the woman beginning her whitewashing, muttering, "The first dirty thing to be removed is one's husband." Twenty-three years before Joseph Hopkinson would pronounce women the more refined sex, this woman put it more bluntly. She called men "naturally nasty beasts; if it were not for their connection with the refined sex . . . these lords of creation would wallow in their own filth."[16]

These fighting words came from a woman who was obviously unimpressed with the Age of Enlightenment. She might have scorned the genteel ladies' salons as much as she did her husband's "philosophical experiments." She did not feel demeaned as a housewife; on the contrary, she considered herself refined because she was sensible, practical, and competent. Even though denigrated by her husband, she did not question the idea of her subordination to him. She did, however, complain about it, and here she represented a dramatic break with the past. Earlier in the century, though they shared many of her values, women did not speak out as she did, at least not publicly. The spirited objections of exploited wives were the first

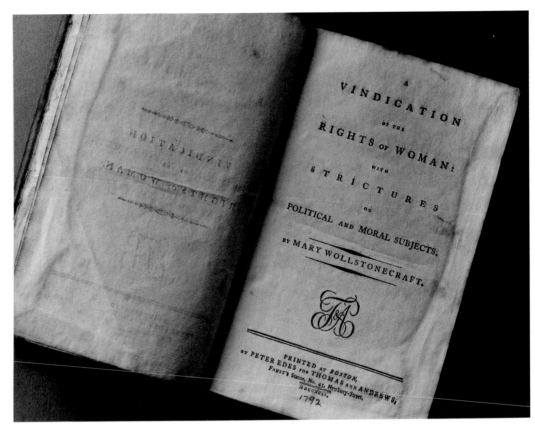

Figure 98. Title page of the American edition of Mary Wollstonecraft's influential book, *A Vindication of the Rights of Woman: With Strictures on Political and Moral Subjects.*

open skirmishes in the full-scale battle of the sexes highlighting this period.

The climate of opinion that fostered even this modest rebellion was a result of several factors. Especially among the affluent, the rhetoric of the American and French Revolutions was absorbed into women's thinking. Orthodox religion, which previously had tended to keep women confined and submissive, lost much of its impact toward the end of the eighteenth century. Rigid religious beliefs about the inferiority of women and the depravity of children slowly softened. New liberal, humanistic influences stressed natural rights and human perfectibility. These new philosophies infused the new government and its affluent constituency with an unprecedented regard for women and children. Supportive men such as the outspoken Benjamin Franklin and Benjamin Rush tried to encourage women to prepare themselves to be intelligent, responsible citizens of the new republic.

The English feminist, Mary Wollstonecraft, led the struggle for women's rights. Her writings attracted a wide and distinguished readership in America, including Martha Washington. An entry for March 31, 1794, in George Washington's account listed *"Wolstoncroft's Education* for Mrs. Washington."[17] In particular, her 1792 book *A Vindication of the Rights of Women*, published in London, Boston, and Philadelphia, attained instant popularity and notoriety. It remains today one of the most influential books ever written about women (figure 98).

Wollstonecraft boldly asserted that men and women had equal abilities; only society's training accounted for the disparity in their achievements. She pleaded for women to be educated in professions, rather than just accomplishments, not so that they would "have power over men, but over themselves." Linking the cause of women to the ideals of democracy and enlightenment, which had spurred revolutions in America and France, she observed that tyrants, whether weak fathers or kings, are always eager to crush reason. She wrote, "Do you [men] not act a similar part when you *force* all women, by denying them civil and political rights, to remain . . . groping in the dark?" She aimed directly at the ideals and rhetoric of the new American republic, rejecting a philosophy of government that proclaimed all men to be equal to each other but superior to women. "If women are to be excluded, without having a voice, from participation of the natural rights of mankind . . . [this is a] flaw in your NEW CONSTITUTION, the first constitution founded on reason," she wrote.[18]

Personal comments in letters and diaries reveal that Mary Wollstonecraft's ideas struck a nerve of truth for both men and women of the day. A woman who called herself "A Matrimonial Republican" wrote in the July 1792 *Ladies Magazine* that she objected to the word *obey* being part of the woman's marriage vow but not of the man's. She argued, "Obedience between a man and wife . . . ought to be mutual." Otherwise, she concluded, the woman became a virtual slave.[19]

In August 1792, in the same issue of the *Ladies Magazine* that favorably reviewed *A Vindication of the Rights of Women* and quoted it liberally, an article entitled "Thoughts on Women" echoed Wollstonecraft's views. The author declared, for example, "To the age of thirteen or fourteen, girls are every where superior to boys. At fourteen a boy begins to get some advantages over a girl . . . by means of education."[20]

Elizabeth Drinker, essentially a conservative and thoughtful woman, entered in her diary of March 6, 1799, "To say the truth, I think her a prodigious fine writer—and should be charmed by some of her pieces if I had never heard her Character." She agreed with many of Wollstonecraft's points but felt, "I am not for quite so much independence."[21] Unfortunately, by this time Wollstonecraft's sympathies for the French Revolution and her scandalous private life gave her the image of a dangerous radical.

All of these discussions and writings apparently produced a change in women's activities. An unidentified "L. C." in the December, 1810 *Port Folio* noted that, "Instead of wasting precious hours of their lives in trifling amusements and petty occupations, the ladies, in a majority of instance, are now profitably employed in the cultivation of their minds. . . . The husband no longer need blush at the folly of his wife, or dread to spend the long evenings of winter in her insipid company."[22]

Real improvements for women progressed very slowly and primarily affected only women of the middling or better sort. Eager as some might have been for a new day, women had no pertinent role models to guide them. To move from a subordinate to an equal role required a great deal of change, and women had no experience in doing so. It was one thing to point out inequities but quite another to conceive of methods to change them. The typical genteel lady of the day was simply not yet ready to abandon, as Wollstonecraft and her followers had urged her to, the age-old belief that nature intended men and women to have completely different roles in life. The stylish lady found the prerogatives of female privilege comforting and reassuring, and the hypothetical state of equality with men threatening and unknown. Gradually, she opted for the new exaltation men offered her: privilege, of a sort, over equality. By the 1820s, the atmosphere of unprecedented regard for women masked a new form of subservience and doomed their demands for equality. To seal the issue, men's attitudes about themselves also underwent change. The ideal of an enlightened, cultured, intellectual man gave way to the new image of man as aggressive and domineering, functioning within the competitive economic system. Men with these

Figure 99. A pair of coats of arms, one a watercolor on paper, the other a silk embroidery on a silk satin weave ground, worked entirely in whip stitch. Both pieces claim to represent the name of Putnam, but these arms are not recorded for Putnam or anyone else. Done by Betsy Putnam. Salem, Massachusetts, 1790–1810. Embroidery: H. 14 1/4"; W. 10 1/8".

attitudes preferred their women exalted and obedient—above and below them, but not equal to them.

☙

DURING THE UNPRECEDENTED period of enlightenment for women at the end of the eighteenth and the beginning of the nineteenth century, the products of women's needlework skills reflected their thoughts and feelings about themselves, just as their clothing did. Still important, fancy samplers vied with fashionable silk pictures which radiated elegance (figure 99). Their bright, shiny silks were more available and less expensive after the Revolutionary War when direct trade between the United States and China began. These pieces complemented the new interiors, which were showier and more delicate. Furniture of lighter-colored woods had shimmering veneered surfaces and elaborate inlays. To enhance their pictures, needleworkers added silver or gold spangles (the eighteenth-century equivalent of sequins; figure 100) and metallic yarns (see Glossary). Chenille yarns (see Glossary) contributed a plush, fuzzy texture. Glittering gold-leafed frames, often with mirror-like black and white reverse painted glass mats, added a final opulent touch (figures 101 and 102).

Coats of arms were another form of fancy work with a long life span. The earliest known American coat of arms is an example of quill work (see Glossary) dated 1693, portraying the arms for Benjamin Smith and now owned by Winterthur Museum. Five years after the first American newspapers started, the *Boston Chronicle* for May 1, 1709, mentioned a school which taught embroidered coats of arms. However, most of the existing examples date from 1750 to 1820. Few were worked outside of New England; those of Ann Flowers (figure 52) and her sister in Philadelphia were exceptions. Most of the early New England embroidered arms were worked with a solid ground in tent stitch (plate 34).

The artist Thomas Cole was well-known in his time for drawing arms (figure 99). His designs are characterized by crossed stalks at the bottom and little nervous squiggles as fillers in the upper section. Figure 99 is a design drawn and worked in watercolors by Cole. It was copied for needle

Figure 100. Needlework picture of Maria, the heroine of Laurence Sterne's novel *A Sentimental Journey*. Worked with silk and a small amount of very fine wool on silk satin weave ground. Stitches are satin, whip, and chain. The chain stitch outlines the oval and holds the spaced silver spangles. Expert painting is on the face and hands. Originally a decorative ribbon was around the edge; it was unfortunately removed. Probably Philadelphia; 1800–1825. H. 23"; W. 26 3/4".

Figure 101. A flower picture finely worked in silk, using satin and whip stitches. Set with a black and gold reverse painted glass mat in its original frame labeled by Stillman Lothrop (an apprentice of John Doggett's; see Figures 107 and 108) of Salem, Massachusetts. H. 20 1/2"; W. 16 9/16".

work in silk and embroidered by Betsy Putnam. Both the colored drawing and the embroidery remain in their original frames. Most prevalent in America were embroidered coats of arms; arms painted on velvet are unusual (figure 87).

The fancy sampler continued to be an essential accomplishment for the eligible young woman to display in her home, and schools continued to produce distinctive designs. In general, these samplers are larger than their eighteenth-century counterparts. Novelties, such as colored grounds (plate 9), map samplers, and globes also appeared.

An exciting group of three samplers, made by two Cooper sisters—Mary and Sarah—and their cousin, Hannah Cooper, all of whom lived in Camden, New Jersey, just across the river from Philadelphia, were discovered together in 1987. They were stitched on a tiffany (see Glossary) ground in tiny silk tent stitches. This meticulous work is typical of earlier embroidery. Although Mary's compartmented sampler (figure 103), still in its original frame, is representative of a style worked in the Philadelphia area, Hannah created a sampler with an oval center (figure 104), a style not previously recognized as a Philadelphia form. Sarah also made an oval design, this with a seated woman in the center, a year later.[23]

An interesting similarity exists between these ovals and samplers with compartmented designs worked about five years later at schools in Lancaster, Pennsylvania, run by twin sisters Leah Galligher and Rachel Bratton Armstrong (figures 105 and 106). Their father was a prosperous farmer in Brandywine Hundred, Delaware, only thirty miles from Philadelphia. The designs invite speculation. Did these sisters also attend Ann Marsh's school or did they adapt designs from Marsh-school examples? Leah remarried and became Leah Maguire after a much publicized and scandalous divorce in Lancaster. She then moved to Harrisburg and resumed teaching using the same patterns. Soon local teachers began to pirate Leah's designs.

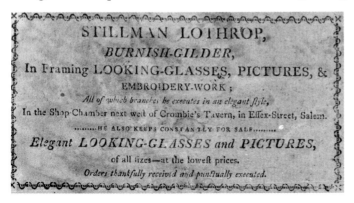

STILLMAN LOTHROP,
BURNISH-GILDER,
In Framing LOOKING-GLASSES, PICTURES, &
EMBROIDERY-WORK ;
All of which branches he executes in an elegant style,
In the Shop-Chamber next west of Crombie's Tavern, in Essex-Street, Salem.
.........HE ALSO KEEPS CONSTANTLY FOR SALE.........
Elegant LOOKING-GLASSES and PICTURES,
of all sizes—at the lowest prices.
Orders thankfully received and punctually executed.

Figure 102 (opposite). Detail of the Stillman Lothrop label. The wording on the label is evidence that many needlework pictures were framed for household decoration.

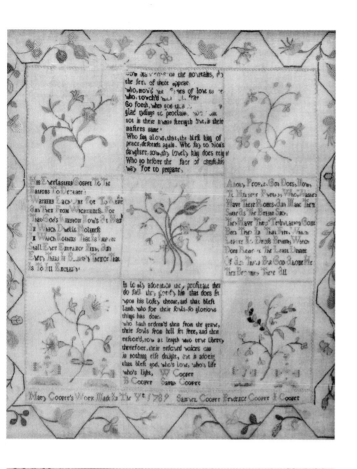

Figure 103 (top left opposite). Mary Cooper's compartmented sampler done in 1789, still in its original frame, has the only currently known inscription identifying this group with Ann Marsh. On the backboard of Mary Cooper's original frame is written in an eighteenth-century hand, "Mary Cooper's Work / done at Ann Marshs school / Philadelphia." Worked in tent, Queen's, flat, cross, and satin stitches on a very fine tiffany ground. H. 18 1/4"; W. 16 1/2". *Collector's Circle Funds.*

Figure 104. (top right opposite). Hannah Cooper, a cousin of Mary, undoubtedly attended Ann Marsh's school, judging from the similarity of materials and workmanship. This piece descended with figure 103 and an oval portraying a seated woman by Sarah Cooper, dated 1792. Hannah's stitches are buttonhole, tent, cross, French knots, and bullion. H. 15 1/2"; W. 13 5/16". *Collector's Circle Funds.*

Figure 105 (bottom left opposite). Made by Martha Taylor in 1797, the year Leah Galligher opened her school in Lancaster, Pennsylvania. The squares in Martha's sampler are related to those in figure 103, only moved to the outside. The tiffany background fabric, silk yarns, and most of the stitches are identical. Martha's direct descendent donated Martha's younger sister's sampler, similarly worked, as well as Martha's marking sampler, dated a year after this, and Martha's silhouette done in Peale's Museum. H. 17 1/2"; W. 18". *Gift of Elizabeth Oat Rockwell.*

Figure 106 (bottom right opposite). An 1805 sampler, by Phebe Bratton, who attended Rachel Armstrong's school in Lancaster, Pennsylvania, demonstrates the similarities to Ann Marsh's oval designs. Here the tiny Vs surround the outside of an oval with the same tiffany ground and tiny sparkling satin, whip, and herringbone stitches. Painting the sky on this sheer fabric was a disaster. H. 16"; W. 16 1/4". *Gift of Miss Elizabeth Hudson.*

Though some needlework schools upheld the old standards of workmanship, many needlework pictures executed around the turn of the century exhibit a gradual decline in excellence from those of the pre-Revolutionary period. There are telling signs of shortcuts. Especially after 1800, faces, skies, and water in many needlework pictures (and a few samplers) were painted in—an embellishment that also saved time. Whereas earlier silk pictures were done in a wide variety of stitches, later silk embroideries consisted primarily of rows of the quicker and easier whip stitches (figures 100, 107, and 109). Compact rows of whip stitches, worked so that stitches of successive rows line up one below the other, create a rippled, shimmering effect especially appropriate for imitating folds of material.[24]

The extravagant and occasionally gaudy appearance and declining workmanship of these needlework pictures demonstrate that school girls were unwilling to do the time-consuming projects of an earlier generation (figures 110 and 111). The subject matter of some of these pictures, however, is novel. They often show a fashionable interest in classical motifs even when portraying scenes from the Bible, popular novels, or most com-

Figure 107. Picture captioned, "And the Daughter of Pharaoh came down to wash herself at the river; and when she saw the Ark among the flags she sent her maid to fetch it. Exod Ch. 2^d Verse 5." On the reverse painted mat with gilt letters: "Wrought by Mary S. Crafts at Mrs Saunder's & Miss. Beach's Academy Dorchester." The inscription on the backboard indicates that Mary was probably seventeen years old when she made this. All the solid needlework areas were done in whip stitch except the two thin trees to the left, which are satin-stitched. The faces, arms, foreground, and background were painted. 1805. H. 16 1/2"; W. 12 3/4".

monly, mourning scenes (plate 35; figure 109). The mourning pictures are particularly sentimental, with long-haired maidens standing soulfully under willow trees—willows were a traditional symbol of mourning. Females of all ages could, and were expected to, indulge in the luxury of sentimentality. The novel, a newly accepted form of literature, depicted and accentuated these tender sentiments. The new feminine virtues included the sensitivity to be touched, even moved to tears, by tragic tales. In sharp contrast, the

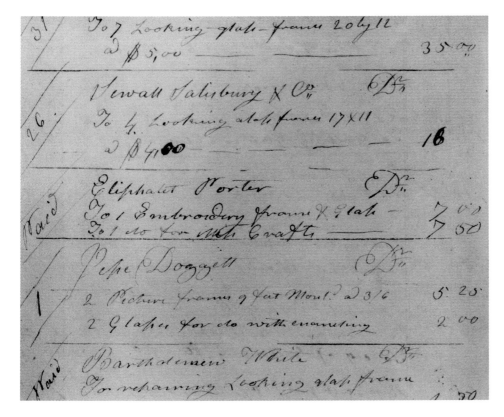

Figure 108. Account book of John Doggett for October 5, 1805, showing a bill to Mary Crafts's uncle, Eliphelet Porter, for two frames, one costing $7.50 specifically for Miss Crafts's embroidery. *DMMC, WM, 64x10, 88.*

girls and women of the earlier era had not been encouraged to contemplate life's cruelties and display them in their crafts. Death had been dealt with directly (figure 112). The sentimental interpretation of death or other natural occurrences was a new practice, partially spurred by the belief that the great role of art should be its impact on the imagination. Such sentimentality had not been previously displayed in needlework. Earlier stitched pictures had displayed bright, cheerful floral designs and scenes.

Until the third quarter of the eighteenth century, people interpreted life as having three phases: birth, marriage, and death. They thought each phase should be considered and experienced in the best way possible. Therefore, it became the practice, particularly for men, to visit an acquaintance who was dying in order to learn about death. Dying became a public event, and letters and diaries often mention visits, recording whether the

Figure 109 (right). A mourning picture with unintended whimsy. Two young women were attractively painted on a silk ground with perfectly coifed hair and costumes. They point up to a collapsing willow tree that looks as if it were caught in a hurricane. This example is still in its original reverse painted glass and frame. Diana Harriet Cogswell of Westboro, Massachusetts, worked this piece and a well-done marking sampler not pictured. Overall frame H. 25 1/2"; W. 21 1/2".
Given in memory of Bessie Maynard Henry.

Figure 110 (opposite). A sampler-picture totally out of character from the usual Wilmington, Delaware, prim Quaker needlework. This sampler by Ingeber R. Vandever, dated 1829, was stitched by a descendent of one of the seventeenth-century founding Swedish families. An almost identical example exists with its maker's name removed but with "Wilmington, Del." Plain silk and chenille yarns in satin, herringbone, French knots, whip, laid, seed, back, star, and cross stitches.
H. 18 3/4"; W. 18 1/4".

Tuition by
A Washington INGEBER R VANDEVER of her age 1829.
work in the 12th year

Figure 111 (top). Most unusual is this painted velvet appliqué, from figure 110, attached to the background with embroidery stitches of the tree foliage and ground.

Figure 112 (bottom). A toy coffin of wood, complete with the glass window some people then favored for actual coffins, to be sure the body was in fact dead. This toy has a small removable carved wooden figure in it.

Figure 113. A large version of Christ rising, signed G. Folwell, demonstrates the growing interest in the New Testament at this time. Several versions of this print are known, drawn both by Godfrey and his father, Samuel, who died in 1813 when Godfrey was only fourteen years old. His mother continued to conduct her school and Godfrey soon provided the designs. M. M. Keating was probably the daughter of John Keating, listed as a gentleman in the directories from 1816 to 1825. H. 26 1/16"; W 34".

Figure 115. A group of mourning pins and rings, for the fashionable display of grief. The coffin-shaped spoon handle became popular during the period of public mourning observed for George Washington, 1800–1810. The Irish-stitched Bible in the background was worked in shades of red, blue, purple, and gold and once belonged to the Philadelphia cabinetmaker John Gillingham. It was stitched probably by his wife, Ann, or daughter Elizabeth. *Three of the mourning rings were the gift of Mrs. George Batchelder. The Washington hair pin was the gift of Mrs. Paul Hammond.*

utmost pleasure; I think it will look best on white sattin . . . But I wish you to chuse a Motto to go in the Urn. If you wish a name let me know and I will do it." Obviously the Akerly mourning piece owed its inspiration strictly to fashion rather than to any personal reason for mourning (plate 35). Similarly, when Eliza Southgate's sister Octavia wrote from Mrs. Rowson's school at Medford, Massachusetts, asking her sister to help select her next needlework project, Eliza replied "About your work . . . a *mourning piece* with a figure in it, and two other pictures, *mates*—figures of females I think handsomer than Landscapes."[25]

George Washington's death, in 1799, provoked a wave of mourning that took many forms. American needleworkers and other craftsmen produced a flood of mourning pictures in honor of Washington, and the President, who when he lived had taken pains not to be treated as a king, was sanctified in death. Few homes in America were without a print, needlework picture, or some other representation of Washington's death. Mourning had become patriotic as well as stylishly sensitive (figures 116 and 117).

Perhaps Mark Twain best summarized this style of sentimentality in *Huckleberry Finn.* By the time Twain was writing, in the last third of the nineteenth century, mourning pictures had gone out of style, but apparently they had made a lasting impression. In one scene Huck confronted a room full of mourning pictures, one of which memorialized even the demise of a bird. Taken aback, Huck reasoned that the person responsible for decorating the room had gloried in her "tributes" to the dead, but he confessed that they only gave him "the fantods."[26]

Paradoxically, these silk mourning pictures embraced classical symbolism while they indulged in romantic sentimentality. Mourning themes with a tomb, weeping willows, and classically clad figures had been used in needlework, memorial jewelry, and prints in America in the 1790s prior to George Washington's death.[27] However, the great emphasis on creating mourning objects occurred between 1800 and 1830 (figure 118). Fashionable women adopted the classical custom of memorializing the dead with tombs and urns, transforming these receptacles of honor into monuments to sentimentality.

The position of women changed during these years, with the

Figure 116 (opposite). The tomb design of this silk work mourning picture was traced from figure 117. The skillful embroiderer used whip, satin, French knots, and seed stitches. The faces, arms, and sky were poorly painted on the silk. Washington's picture was painted on paper and appliquéed to the tomb. A linen strip with eyelet holes, used to lace the embroidery in a sewing frame, is still attached. United States; 1800–1810. H. 15 1/4"; W. 16 3/4".

Figure 117 (top). Etching titled *Pater Patriae* by Enoch G. Gridley, based on a painting by John Coles, Jr. The portrait medallion of George Washington was copied from the one painted by Edward Savage. 1800. H. 13 1/2"; W. 9 1/2".

Figure 118 (bottom). This print clearly shows that by 1831 larger stones, obelisks, tombs, and urns were more fashionable monuments. Only one small stone remains for sale. Picture of the Franklin Marble Mantel Manufactory in Philadelphia, located on Race Street between Sixth and Seventh Streets. From Thomas Porter's *Picture of Philadelphia from 1811 to 1831*, published in Philadelphia in 1831 by Robert Desilver . *DMMC, WM, F158.44P54me, v*

exhuberant optimism of the revolutionary age receding while a more restrictive, sentimental outlook on life set in. Perhaps the popularity of needlework mourning pictures conveys some awareness on the part of this class of women of their altered status. Put another way, women buried the idea of their enlightenment in its own symbols.

NOTES

1. Hopkinson, "Address to Pennsylvania Academy," 34.
2. Livingston, *Nancy Shippen*, 220–21.
3. Thomson, "Letters," 35.
4. Emery, *Reminiscences*, 245.
5. Franks, "Letter of Rebecca Franks," 304.
6. Emery. *Reminiscences*, 246.
7. Hutson, "Women in the Era," 297.
8. Herr. "Moravian Schoolgirl Needlework," 315.
9. Diary of Elizabeth Drinker. May 4, 1778.
10. Birthing chairs were an ubiquitous form in Europe and England from the middle ages and were also used in America.
11. Hopkinson, "Address to Pennsylvania Academy," 34.
12 Harris, "Gilbert Stuart," 210.
13. [Farrar], *Young Lady's Friend,* 97.
14. Vanderpoel, *Chronicles,* 36. Watson, *Annals,* 176.
15. More, *Strictures,* vol. 1, 86.
16. Nitidia, "Letter to the Editor," 375–377.
17. "Washington's Household Account Book," 173.
18. Wollstonecraft, *Vindication,* 189-190
19. Matrimonial Republican, "On Matrimonial Obedience," 66.
20. "Thoughts on Women," 112.
21. Drinker diary, March 6, 1799; April 22, 1796.
22.. L .C., "Ladies of Philadelphia," 606.
23. Swan, "Recent Discoveries," 1340.
24. These silk pieces are often called satin stitch pictures today, but the author has discovered that what appears on the front to be satin stitches are, usually in this period, rows of whip stitches.
25. Letter of Margaretta Akerly, March 23, 1796. Bowne, *Girl's Life,* 25.
26. Twain. *Huckleberry Finn,* 137–39.
27. Deutsch, "Washington Memorial Prints," 324–331.

5 To Make a House a Home: *The Age of Domesticity*

Figure 119 (opposite). Purse and eyeglass case using the soft limp merino yarns in Irish stitch. Purse: United States, 1830–1870. H. 6 1/8"; W. 6 1/2". Eyeglass case; H 6 1/8"; W. 2".

SENTIMENTAL, GENTEEL, AND too unsure of themselves to press their earlier claims of equality with men, American women wound up on a less-than-honorable pedestal, glorified for their refinement but firmly limited to a life of domesticity, self-sacrifice, and submission. Instead of gaining power "over themselves," as Wollstonecraft had urged, women assumed the position of moral guardian of the family and allowed this elevated status to mask their continued inferior position. Society righteously insisted that the natures of men and women differed greatly; therefore, their roles should be separate and distinct. Women accepted this view. They sought and received praise for their supposedly unique virtues of passivity, delicacy, obedience, patience, and moral purity, whereas men were lauded for their strength, aggression, and sense of adventure. The unpublished diary of a young Boston woman professed in 1827 that "the sphere of a woman's usefulness ought to be chiefly confined to her family and friends."[1] While the typical husband actively participated in the outside world, his wife operated in a passive sphere of domesticity.

This role for women was rooted in the social and economic practices of the dawning industrial age. Even before the start of the nineteenth century, the urban husband's place of employment began to move outside the home. When it did, the woman of the house could no longer function as her husband's partner in the closely linked home and business affairs of the family, thereby maintaining a limited parity with him. The new economic system separated home from business and husband from wife. The man became the provider, the woman the homemaker.

The post-colonial period of enlightenment had softened these new restrictions by permitting women to loosen their ties to the home without breaking them. However, as the commercial ferment of industrial development overwhelmed the cultural sensibilities of the Age of Enlightenment, women were thrust back into the home again. Man assumed the role of a

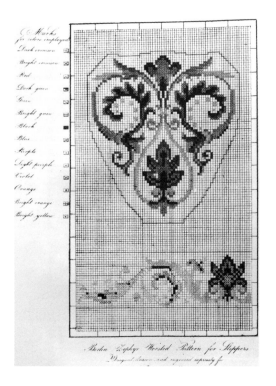 

warrior in the working world who depended on his wife to prepare a sanctuary for him. Woman, with her refinement and sensitivity, was deemed not only well-suited for the task of haven-making but ennobled by it. In her home she reigned over children, virtue, faith, taste—all things that, like herself, had little or no place in a man's world of business.

The Second Great Awakening, an evangelical religious movement that swept the United States early in the nineteenth century, helped create this new role for women. The clergy so assiduously cultivated women by praising their moral virtues that Mrs. Frances Trollope, the caustic English travel writer, observed, "[I]t is from the clergy only that women of America receive the sort of attention which is so dearly valued by every young female heart throughout the world." Meanwhile, the clergy rarely reached men, who considered themselves too busy earning a living to be concerned with moral preachments. Mrs. Trollope observed, "I never saw, or read, of any country where religion had so strong a hold upon the women, or a slighter hold upon the men."[2]

The press joined the pulpit in its crusade to appoint women society's moral guardians. Women in America had never lacked instruction from printed materials on how to behave, but after 1830, the amount of published material greatly increased, spurred by the growing literacy rate among women, an increase in their leisure time, and the invention of lower-cost printing machinery. Spiritual sustenance became available to women of all economic levels via newspapers, manner books, and magazines. The pioneer American magazine in ladies' how-to literature was *The Lady's Book*, started in 1830 by Louis A. Godey and soon known as *Godey's Lady's Book*. It offered among other items short moralistic stories and the editorial exhortations of its editor, Sarah Josepha Hale. Other such magazines as *Miss Leslie's Magazine* and Miss *Peterson's National Magazine* soon chimed in.

Even daily newspapers served as advisers to women. On November 28, 1827, a "Code of Instructions for Ladies " in the *Baltimore American and Commercial Daily Advertiser* summarized society's expectations of its women:

1. Let every wife be persuaded that there are two ways of governing a family; the first is by the expression of that will which belongs to force; the second by the power of mildness. One is the power of the husband; the wife should never employ any other arms than gentleness.
2. Avoid contradicting your husband. . . .
3. Occupy yourself only with your household affairs. . . .
4. Never take upon yourself to be a censor of your husband's morals. . . .
5. Command his attention by being always attentive to him.
6. All men are vain, never wound this vanity. . . . A wife may have more sense than her husband, but she should never seem to know it.
7. When a man gives wrong counsel, never make him feel that he has done so. . . .
8. When a husband is out of temper, behave obligingly to him. . . .
9. Choose well your female friends; have but few. . . .
10. Cherish neatness without luxury, and pleasure without excess; dress with taste, and particularly with modesty. . . .
11. Never be curious to pry into your husband's concerns. . . .
12. Seem always to obtain information from him, especially before

company, though you may pass yourself for a simpleton. Never forget that a wife owes all her importance to that of her husband.—Leave him entirely master of his actions, to go and come whenever he thinks fit.

A woman had always been considered a jewel in her husband's crown. Now she found herself expected to be his benefactress as well, restraining herself and even practicing deceit to cater to his sense of superiority. She had little choice, for she depended on her husband more than ever. She was his to honor or exploit. In the editorial "Advice to a Bride " in *The Lady's Book* for May, 1832, Sarah Hale warned, "Your duty is submission. . . . Your husband is, by the laws of God and of man, your superior; do not ever give him a cause to remind you of it."[3]

Sometimes a woman attempted to make an asset of her dependence, flattering her husband with her vulnerability, but this was a dangerous ploy. Frances Wright, a perceptive Englishwoman who visited America, found that men thought it pleasing to have as "their companion a fragile vine, clinging to their firm trunk for support." Yet these same vines, she realized, often "weighed the oak to the ground."[4] Women had to be submissive without being burdensome, a delicate balance to maintain.

Girls who had grown up with the romantic expectation that in marriage they would be completely cared for by men had to learn how to cultivate this privileged state. The life of a woman developed into an unending mission to endear herself to her husband to "preserve a perpetual charm," as Mrs. Hale put it, for "the nature of man is such, that where there is no excitement, there he is faithless. . . . The ardour of man's dispositions leads him to very romantic professions . . . without doubt sincerely intended—but he professes more than humanity can accomplish." To allow her husband to feel free and yet to keep him coming back to her, a wife strove to give him what he wanted and to make as few demands on him as possible. She was admonished not to meddle in his affairs, not to burden him in any way because he already carried the burdens of business. He wanted a tranquil refuge from the worries of the working world, and she was to devote herself to creating it. Mrs. Hale counseled, "Let all your enjoyment centre in your home. Let your home occupy the first place in your thoughts; for that is the

Plate 36 The giving of a quilting party, especially in rural areas, was similar in purpose to an engagement announcement today. This unsigned painting, by John Lewis Krimmel, was completed in 1813. It illustrates that after the quilt had been finished, the invited guests arrived to enjoy a dinner and perhaps dancing.

Plate 37 A large appliquéed quilt using English roller-printed chintzes of the 1830s. The quilting itself, done in a very fine running stitch, creates a texture. United States; 1835–1845. H. 123"; W. 118 3/4".

only source of happiness."[5]

To be sure, a few women, especially those who had a received good education, did choose alternatives to the life of a housewife. Against great odds and adversity, they pursued careers, usually at the cost of being all but ostracized by society. There was often no middle ground of having both a family and a profession. Victorian society considered homemaking a woman's highest calling, and for the society to have permitted women both marriage and a career would have implied that homemaking was less than totally fulfilling. If she chose a career, a woman had to be prepared to sacrifice marriage and a family, and, like spinsters all through the years, endure ridicule.

In professional life, the few exceptions needed skill, endurance, courage, and luck to succeed. In 1847 Elizabeth Blackwell became the first female medical student in the country by gaining admittance to Geneva College in New York. Administrators, taken aback by an application from a female, decided to poll the student body to determine whether a woman should be accepted. The students refused to believe that a woman was really applying and, thinking it all a joke, voted to admit her.

Of the overwhelming majority of women who remained in the home, some aspired to a semiprofessional level of competence in their homemaking, stimulated by the teachings of such leading educators as Catherine Beecher. Beecher stressed the importance of the family as the foundation of the social order. By promoting the happiness and well-being of the family, women helped shape a virtuous society.[6] Her 1841 *Treatise on Domestic Economy* gave clear, sensible advice on all facets of homemaking, including the architectural design of the house. Her practical approach did more to elevate the status of the housewife than all the flowery rhetoric about women's virtues. However, on the whole, sentimentality and a new womanly virtue, propriety, overwhelmed practicality and competence as ideals for women.

The Victorian lady's activities outside the home centered on church activities, visiting, and shopping. The wife continued and in many cases expanded her rounds of visiting. Calling was no longer always done for the gaiety of it—it had become almost a chore—but to uphold her social position

and, by inevitable extension, that of her husband. The calling cards she left behind served, according to *The Young Lady's Friend* (1837), "to keep up a ceremonious acquaintance with a circle too large for friendly visiting, as that consumes far more time than could be given to the number of persons you must be acquainted with."[7]

The busy husband turned over much of the household purchasing to his wife. Diaries and contemporary remarks show that shopping, but not necessarily purchasing, became a pastime for many of these idle women. Servants became essential to supply the leisure time for shopping and visiting. Even if they could barely afford it, husbands often felt obliged by their social position to hire at least a cook and maid for the household. Management of this help added another necessary skill to the new domesticity.

Victorian housewives with time to fill, hands to keep busy, and homes to prettify became zealous needleworkers. They made innumerable household accessories, covering anything that did not move, and a few things that did—slippers, wastebaskets, ottomans, picture frames, cigar cases, pillows, tables, bell pulls, valances for mantels, needle cases, and antimacassars. And now, thanks again to the less-expensive printing machinery, almost every woman could learn to do fancy needlework. No longer did women need special tutoring from needlework teachers. The same magazines that a woman relied on for guidance about proper behavior plied her with needlework patterns and instructions for projects that were all well within the capabilities of the average housewife.

Starting in the 1840s, needlework books appeared en masse, further popularizing fancy needlework. From posterity's standpoint, these books made their greatest contribution in further obfuscating needlework terminology, as if it were not already confusing enough. Probably in an effort to distinguish their books from those of the competition, the authors took to making tiny variations on well-known stitches and then renaming the stitches, often with elegant-sounding foreign names. Sometimes they simply changed the name of a stitch without bothering to change the stitch itself.

Figure 122 (opposite). Samplers were larger and displayed coarser work after 1830 to 1835. By 1843, few girls worked fancy samplers at all. Here M. E. England displays an interesting mixture of influences: the two baskets, facing birds, and the vines on either side of and below her name and date show a Quaker influence. The ribbon border was typical of earlier Delaware Valley work, and the rest of the elements are common to Berlin work. It was stitched in merino yarn on a finer ground than is typical of its day. Pennsylvania or Maryland. H. 21 7/8"; W. 19". *Gift in memory of Miss Helen E. Lynch.*

The great vogue in needlework during the Victorian period was Berlin work (see Glossary), a form that took its name from its origins. About 1804, a print seller in Berlin, Germany, A. Philipson, had the idea of making paper with intersecting lines (similar to graph paper) to correspond to a canvas background. He then had designs hand painted on this paper for the needleworker to copy onto her canvas. She could transfer the design, square for square, in whatever stitch she chose—usually cross or tent but occasionally Irish. She did not even have to bother with color selection, or shading as needlework instructors had called it, because the paper pattern came already colored (figure 120). After 1830, American magazines and books substituted symbols or numbers for the hand-colored squares.

Berlin work became so popular that the manufacturers of canvases adapted their products to it, using a white, yellow, or blue thread every tenth space on the canvas to enable the needle woman to count squares more easily and thus transfer the design from the pattern more quickly (figure 121). Another innovation in canvas, developed in the mid-nineteenth century and still popular today, is Penelope, or Berlin canvas. It consists of doubled warp and weft threads, which allow the needleworker to separate the paired threads and thereby work fine details of the design. In general, however, background canvases became coarser than they had been in the eighteenth century. One rarely finds Victorian canvas work finer than twenty-four holes to the inch. It was, after all, not by demanding fine workmanship that Berlin work established its popularity. Its appeal lay rather in its convenience, like other products of the Industrial Revolution. It did require patience but very little skill and no creativity. Victorian women distinguished themselves by the quantity rather than the quality of their needlework. In 1840, in her book *The Art of Needle-Work from Earliest Times*, the Countess of Wilton wrote, "Of the fourteen thousand Berlin patterns which have been published, [in the ten years since 1830] scarcely one-half are moderately good."[8]

Before 1830, most American needle women used crewel or silk yarns, sometimes combined with beads, to work the printed Berlin patterns. After 1830, softer, angora-like merino yarns gradually found their way into Berlin work and samplers (figure 122). In the United States fancy samplers were all but abandoned by 1845. Between 1800 and 1810, the United States witnessed a fad for merino wool, and the price of these purebred sheep rose sharply. Domestic yarns became available soon afterward, but they did not gain a competitive advantage over imported yarns for quite some time (figure 119).

In dyeing merino yarns, the Germans at first outshone the British, who previously had been the wool specialists. These new yarns came to be called Berlin, German, or zephyr wools. An entry from the Moravian School in Bethlehem, Pennsylvania, discloses that even this school, famous for its fine fancy needlework, succumbed to Berlin work's overwhelming popularity. In 1839, John G. Kummer purchased for the school "Zephyr" yarn, canvas, and patterns by number from the New York City firm A. S. Schrader.[9]

The most popular yarns were of vivid colors, made even more intense after the invention of the synthetic dye aniline in 1858. Many of these new dyes proved fugitive, and as a result many pieces of Berlin work that survive today have changed color and faded badly, leaving us only pale renditions of the strident color schemes that were considered fashionable during the mid-nineteenth century. Strong maroons, purples, pinks, and oranges clashed with equally strong greens and blues. The Countess of Wilton wrote that Berlin work "seems to have been [meant] to produce a glare of colour rather than the subdued but beautiful effect" of the Gobelin tapestries that this work was meant to imitate.[10]

Later in the nineteenth century, Mark Twain wrote about Berlin work with some irreverence. In *Life on the Mississippi*, he described a needlework picture of "'Washington Crossing the Delaware' . . . done in thunder-and-lightning crewels by one of the young ladies—[a] work of art which would have made Washington hesitate about crossing, if he could have foreseen what advantage was going to be taken of it."[11]

In addition to depictions of historical events, Berlin work designs based on Biblical and Shakespearean themes, all calling for similarly gaudy color schemes, sold well. The Victorian woman had a taste for sentimentality that was more pronounced than that of her predecessors. To enhance a serene little nest for herself and her family, she favored needlework designs that promoted this rose-colored view of the world. Mottoes such as "God bless this home" added a final precious touch to her needlework.

In time, this needlework, like the life it epitomized, often became more stultifying than rewarding. Not even the continued urgings of the magazines, hinting that yet another trifle would further sanctify her place in the home, could keep the housewife producing Berlin work indefinitely. By 1860 or 1870, the great quantity and low quality of such work in most homes became the subject of derisive magazine articles, and women tried to find new ways to demonstrate their domestic devotion.

At least one escape could provide a reliable respite from the tedium of domesticity: the company of other women. Many women drawn to the religious reawakening and pietistic movements for solace, inspiration, and support also found satisfaction in the ensuing companionship and interaction with other women. This sort of socializing should not to be confused with the perfunctory social calls of the time in which women used each other to keep up appearances. Here women had the chance to form meaningful friendships in an atmosphere of Christian kindliness and charity. Around the start of the nineteenth century, men's and women's interests had converged, allowing women a tentative foothold in the male social world. Now thoroughly excluded from the male world, women opted for the company of other women as a relief from the burdens of marriage and motherhood. Women had always sought each other out, but now they had a greater need for their companionship than ever before.

A different but equally satisfying reason to congregate came on the occasions when a woman was ready to finish a quilt. Quilting (see Glossary) readily lent itself to numerous hands and festive affairs (plate 36). An invitation to a quilting party often signified the engagement of the hostess. The bride-to-be would invite her female friends to help her put the finishing touches on quilt tops that she had been preparing for her future home. At the end of the day or days of quilting, the local young men arrived for a meal and perhaps dancing. Then they escorted the young women home.

Women brought small pieces for their quilt tops with them to work on while visiting. The many hours required to stitch the top to its interlining and backing allowed women lengthy, unhurried times together, during which they could share their feelings and strengthen friendships. Quilt making did not begin in the Victorian era any more than the socializing it

Figure 123. Detail of the composition of a typical quilt, showing the decorated top, padding, and plain bottom with running stitch pattern. A heavy layer of cotton-wool padding made the quilt warmer but made intricate stitchery more difficult to do. In this example, English copperplate and roller-printed fabrics have been cut out and carefully appliquéed to the top in a blind whip stitch. United States; 1790–1810. H. 92"; W. 103 1/2".

encouraged among women. But like the socializing, quilting attained its greatest importance during this period.

The first settlers brought quilted petticoats to the colonies from England; the first quilts made here were adapted from those of their homeland. During the eighteenth century, quilt making flourished; however, since it was considered plain work it was rarely mentioned in the offerings of needlework teachers. Perhaps to earn extra money, a few teachers mentioned that they would take in quilting, even though they did not teach it. During the nineteenth century, home quilt making increased among women of all social levels except the well-to-do, who could afford to buy ready-made quilts or other types of bed coverings. Women of the middling sort produced most of our surviving quilts. These "show" quilts lasted because they were saved for company, whereas the more common utility quilts that people used regularly for warmth eventually wore out. Appliquéed "friendship quilts," which come from this era, are some of the most interesting to be found today (figure 130).

Quilting is the process of sewing together three separate layers of fabric: the top, the filling, and the lining (figure 123). The filling is usually cotton batting, called cotton-wool, or occasionally, it is simply a worn blanket. The nature of the top layer determines the type of quilt—one-piece, pieced, or appliquéed (see Glossary).

Quilts with one-piece tops were the earliest made in America. Usually their ornamentation derived not so much from the fabric as from the design and the fineness of the stitches fastening the three layers together. During the eighteenth century, women quilted petticoats in this style, the finest ones being made of silk (figure 124). Elizabeth Drinker, for example, recorded on August 26, 1763, that she had "put a Gown skirt in ye Frame, to Quilt this Afternoon." Four days later she added, "Sister and self finish'd my Quilt this afternoon."[12] (Quilting frames were relatively inexpensive. Because they occupied much space, they were usually left up only when in use.) Bodices, jackets, men's vests, and coats for both men and women are other examples of items made using one-piece quilting. Once in a while, the one-piece top consisted of a fabric with a printed pattern, such as an Indian tree of life, instead of a plain-colored fabric. In these cases the seamstress usually decided not to compete with the dominant design and joined the layers together in a simple diamond or a chevron pattern, instead of the customary elaborate stitching.

The second type of quilt, the pieced quilt, is often a utility one. The seamstress aligned the edge of adjacent shapes cut from fabric, stitched them with a running stitch near the edges, and then pressed the raw edges toward the filling layer. Pieced quilting was not difficult if the edges of the pieces were straight (figures 125 and 126). Curved pieces were used infrequently because they were apt to stretch out of shape when sewn together, making the task more vexing.

Naturally enough, the best clues to the date and origin of a pieced quilt come from the fabrics used. The early pieced quilt in figure 125 is a virtual textile sample book for the period from 1780 to 1800.

On an appliquéed quilt the top layer of the quilt is embellished by applying material to it. In the earliest form of appliqué work, the needle

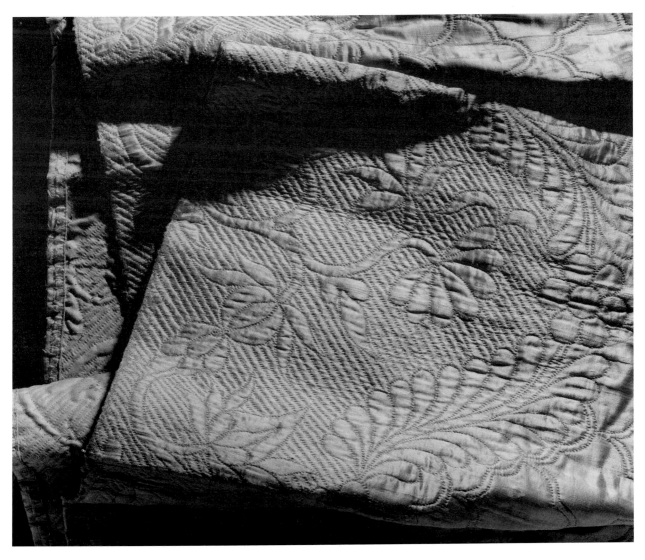

Figure 124. One-piece quilted petticoat, made of pink silk satin weave ground has exotic flowers stitched in very fine running stitches. Originally owned by a member of the Barker family of Scituate, Massachusetts; 1760–1785. H. 36 3/4"; W. around hem 110 1/2".

woman cut out designs from a printed fabric—a bird, for example—leaving one-quarter-inch to one-eighth-inch margins around the figure. She then turned under the raw edges of the cutout pieces to prevent raveling and arranged the pieces on a large background fabric, which would become the top layer of the quilt. Finally, she affixed the pieces to the background fabric with a blind whip stitch or a decorative stitch such as the chain or buttonhole stitch (figure 127). The most exacting and rarest quilting technique was

called inlaid work (see Glossary). Parts of the top layer were cut away, the raw edges turned under, and contrasting-color pieces were stitched underneath in their stead.

Some of the especially adept early quilters created an interesting texture by embroidering the background areas between the appliquéed pieces so finely and tautly that these sections appear delicately puckered (plate 37).

In a similar, though later, nineteenth-century form of appliqué quilting, the needleworker determined the shape of the cutout herself, rather than adopting a design from a fabric. She used a paper or tin pattern (figure 128), in the shape of a star for example, usually favoring plain-colored fabrics or very even, tiny prints. Again she left margins around the cutout pieces, folded the edges underneath to prevent raveling, and stitched the pieces to a background fabric, usually with a blind whip stitch. This completed the top layer of her quilt. Friendship quilts, usually made from appliqué work of this type, combined the squares of cutout material from many different seamstresses, each of whom wrote, stamped, or stitched her name into her contribution (figures 129 and 130). Actual quilting lines could be made from carved wood or metal patterns using chalk to transfer the design to the fabric.

Often a quilt that appears to have been made from just one technique reveals several others on closer inspection. Most of these techniques were so common to our forebears that if a woman mentioned them at all she did not distinguish between, for example, pieced and appliqué work. However, inlaid work, because it was so intricate, did merit special mention by name, as when William Obryen in the *Georgia Gazette* for November 2, 1774, offered "FORTY SHILLINGS REWARD—Stolen . . . A BED QUILT . . . the middle a large tree (inlaid work) with a peacock at the root." In the nineteenth and twentieth centuries women gave names to different designs, but these names often varied from region to region, resulting today in confusing nomenclature.

With a few exceptions, such as inlaid work, quilting, like Berlin work, was simple even though time-consuming. Most quilts were done with just the basic running stitch; very few included many of the fancywork embroidery stitches. But unlike the strictly decorative Berlin work, quilts

Figure 125 (opposite). A one-piece quilt created from a once brilliantly colored, Indian hand painted and resist-dyed printed fabric. In one corner of the fabric is the original stamp of the English East India Company. Originally owned by the Augustine Boyer family of Kent County, Maryland. 1700–1760. H. 111 1/4"; W. 87 1/2". *Gift of Miss Gertrude Brinkle.*

Figure 126. A trundle bed with a silk pieced quilt, featuring a variety of woven, embroidered, yarn-dyed, and hand-painted fabrics. Each piece was first backed with a piece of newspaper. Some show dates of 1788, 1789, and 1790. The paper stiffener made it easier to work with small pieces of silk. Attributed to Martha Agry Vaughn of Hallowell, Maine. 1800–1820. H. 100"; W. 104".

served practical functions. Old ones were sometimes hung in doorways and windows to cut down on drafts, or suspended from attic or lean-to beams as room dividers. In 1835, the inventory of Susan Ward showed that she owned "1 [pair of] dimity quilt curtains."[13] According to John Fanning Watson, quilts served to delineate market stalls on fair days in Philadelphia.

Also unlike Berlin work, which was basically copy stitching, quilts allowed the needleworker to be creative, almost a forgotten word among women in the Victorian era. Some quilts display delicate and refined taste in their subtle blending of colors and prints; others are vigorous and bold, with large pieces and almost clashing color schemes. All captured something of the individual personality of the maker. The considerable amount of time it took to make a quilt gave a woman reason to associate some very personal feelings with it. She might have done one part of it while awaiting the birth

Figure 127 (overleaf). A superb star quilt with the following legend sewn on the back: "Pieced by Mary J Moore in 1837 / Quilted in 1839-Mary j M. Eastburn. It consists of 8437 Pieces." Carefully planned plain, flowered, polka dotted, and striped fabrics were used in consistent order. The quilting follows the edges of the small pieces, but the larger areas are quilted in flower and leaf forms. Mary Jane Moore descended from the Quaker family that founded Moorestown, New Jersey, where she did the piecing in 1837. She married a Delawarean in 1838 and finished her quilting in Delaware in 1839. She lived to be at least ninety-six and bore ten children. H. 110"; W. 107".

Figure 128 (right). A quilt displaying a variety of techniques: embroidered accents, pieced triangles and bands, appliquéed flowers and figures, and stuffed and corded foliage and flowers. In the center scene, blue silk and beige linen threads have been used to appliqué the figures and tree in several variations of the buttonhole stitch. United States, 1820–1834. H. 82 3/4" W. 96".

of a baby, another while a son was off to war. These personal experiences could return to her as she looked at the finished product. Quilts were no paeans to sentimentality; they were chronicles of real life.

It is ironic that quilts represent an era in the history of American women that was on the whole as repressive as the quilts themselves were creative. The progress of women in America has not been continuous or without setbacks, and the Victorian age produced at least as many setbacks as advances.

224 Chapter 5

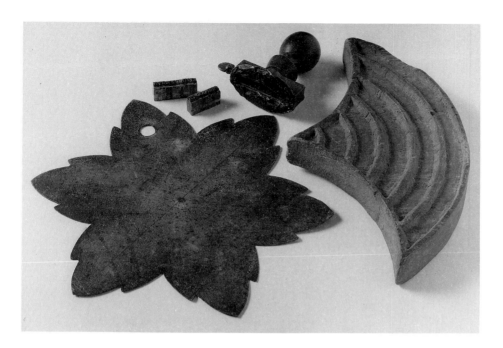

Figure 129. A group of nineteenth-century tools used with quilting. Far right is a carved wooden quilt pattern. The flat metal pattern helped quilters cut out consistently-shaped pieces for appliqué quilts. Women used the small upper tool with a wooden handle and changeable numbers and letters to mark quilt squares and/or household textiles. This pewter casting also printed two facing love birds, laurel leaves, and two hearts pierced with an arrow around the name. Marking stamps were made only after the discovery of an ink that would last and not rot fabric. H. 2 3/8"; W. 2 3/8". *Stamp donated by Mr. and Mrs. Endsley P. Fairman.*

Victorian propriety made it less likely that a woman would consume herself in continual child bearing, but Victorian industrial "progress" forced many poorer women into factories where gruesome working conditions consumed them almost as brutally. Among those women whose husbands' wealth allowed them to stay in the home, the Beechers, the Susan B. Anthonys, and their followers were the rare, able exceptions. The strictures of Victorian society encapsulated women's abilities, which the previous age had just begun to recognize. Painstakingly, women would rediscover and expand their vision of what they could do and would be. In the process, however, most fancy needlework lost its preeminent place as women's most creative mode of expression. The product of a simpler, pre-industrial age, fancy needlework was smothered in Victorian domesticity. Later generations of women, perhaps in admiration of what their colonial forebears had wrought, revived the skills, creatively adapting stitches and designs to contemporary purposes.

Figure 130 (opposite). Mary Simon of Baltimore, recently identified as the person who cut and basted squares for others to work, probably created at least six of the more elaborate squares on this appliquéed Baltimore quilt. A few flowers are three-dimensional with the petals attached only at their centers or bases; others have inked or silk embroidered details. The name of the donor is on each square. H. 122 5/8"; W. 106 1/2".

NOTES

1. Manuscript diary of Hannah Rogers, August 3, 1827.
2. Trollope, *Domestic Manners*, 103–104.
3. [Hale], "Advice to a Bride," 288.
4. Frances Wright, *Views of Society and Manners*, 393.
5. [Hale], "Advice to a Bride," 288–289.
6. Schuyler, *English and American Cottages*, 4145.
7. [Farrar], *Young Lady's Friend*, 390.
8. Countess of Wilton, *Art of Needle-Work*, 398.
9. Accounts of the school, John G. Kummer, July 6, 1839.
10. Countess of Wilton, *Art of Needle-Work*, 398–399.
11. Twain, *Life* , 400.
12. Diary of Elizabeth Drinker, August 26. 1763; August 30, 1763.
13. Inventory of Susan Ward. Dorchester. Mass. June 25, 1835.

Glossary

The aim of this glossary is to help the reader make sense of the rather complex needlework terminology existing today. It attempts to note the relative importance of the different techniques and stitches along with the approximate dates of their greatest popularity. When more than one meaning is in common use for a term, preference has been given to the earliest American meaning that the author could discover in primary sources. Even during the eighteenth century more than one term was occasionally used to describe a stitch or a technique. From the mid-nineteenth century to the present, the number of needlework terms has increased enormously. This proliferation was fueled by the many inexpensive magazines, beginning in the 1830s, and needlework books, in the 1840s, which brought knowledge of fancy needlework to embroiderers in all economic brackets. As the authors of *Art in Needlework*, Lewis Day and Mary Buckle, expressed it in 1900,

> *Each names it after his or her individual discovery . . . and so we have any number of names for the same stitch, which to different people stand often for quite different stitches. When this confusion is complicated by the invention of a new name for every conceivable combination of threads-strokes, or for each slightest variation upon an old stitch—the task of reducing them seems almost hopeless.*

A few needlework patterns were advertised in the several short-lived women's magazines published in the United States between 1790 and 1830. It was not until 1830 with the arrival of *Godey's Lady's Book* that patterns and instructions for their execution regularly appeared in print. The earliest needlework book known to have been used in the United States was *The Art of Needle-Work*, edited by the Countess of Wilton, and published in London in 1840. Unfortunately for researchers, advertisements placed by needlework teachers in American newspapers rarely mentioned or identified specific stitch names.

Textile terminology can get quite confusing. Take for example the simple satin stitch. Over the course of history, it, and its subtle variations, has been described variously as flat, shining, surface satin, Oriental, economy, Roman, Roumanian couching, or whip stitch. Because of this inherent confusion, all related satin stitch techniques are presented under the generic term FLAT STITCH.

The accompanying drawings are intended more to clarify and identify stitches and techniques than to provide how-to-do-it instructions.

APPLIQUÉ WORK; APPLIQUÉ QUILTS: Nineteenth-century terms for the sewing of one or more small pieces of fabric, in geometric or representational shapes, laid on top of a larger background fabric to create a design or picture. Usually, one of three methods was used: (1) a design element, such as a tree or bird, was cut from a printed fabric, with edges turned under, and stitched to the background (this method acquired the name BRODERIE PERSE in the late nineteenth century); (2) a paper or tin pattern was used for cutting the shape of the fabric to be added; or (3) rarely, part of the background fabric was removed in a desired shape and another fabric was added from underneath to fill the area (known then as the inlaid method; today it is usually called reverse appliqué). When the needleworker backed the completed appliquéed piece with an interlining and lining and stitched the layers together, it then became an appliquéed quilt. Example: plate 37; figures 127 and 128.

BACK STITCH: The name of an embroidery stitch included in John Taylor's 1640 poem "In Praise of the Needle" This stitch creates a fine continuous line on the front. It was sometimes used for stuffed and corded work as well as for making fine scrolling lines in embroidery. Example: figure 46.

Back stitch

BARGELLO STITCH: Another name for IRISH STITCH. It did not appear in American needlework books as a substitute for the earlier term Irish stitch until the twentieth century.

BED RUGS: Called "rough woollen coverlets for beds" in Noah Webster's 1806 *Compendious Dictionary*, these were handmade rugs that are easily mistaken for hooked rugs. Running stitches with evenly raised loops of yarn were set very densely in bold patterns on blanket wool. Made during the eighteenth or early nineteenth centuries, many originated in the Connecticut River Valley. Machine-made bed rugs were common, but few have survived. Examples: plate 30; figure 63.

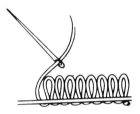

Bed rug

BERLIN NEEDLEWORK: See DRESDEN WORK.

BERLIN WORK: A system of transferring printed paper patterns for needlework designs to canvas. These patterns were published in Germany in the early nineteenth century, and the finished pieces came to be called Berlin work. By the mid-nineteenth century, it was the most popular needlework form in America. Examples: figures 119, 120, and 121.

BERLIN YARN: Also called ZEPHYR, GERMAN, or MERINO YARN and used primarily for CANVAS WORK during the nineteenth century. Spun from the fleece of the merino sheep, a Spanish breed imported into the United States early in the nineteenth century, the yarn has a soft, angora-like feel. Berlin dyers were considered the world's finest, creating nearly a thousand shades for this wool. In the *Spooner & Teale Brooklyn City Directory for 1848-1849*, Mrs. Atkins said she sold German yarns. Example: figure 119.

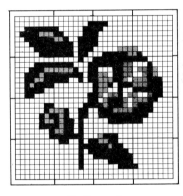

Berlin work

BLOND LACE: An eighteenth-century term for BOBBIN LACE made of silk thread. "Blond" or "blonde" referred to the color of the undyed silk. Advertisements mentioning blond lace (it also was made in black thread) show it was usually imported, but Mrs. Cozani, "lately from London," advertised in *Rivington's New York Gazeteer* for July 28, 1774, that she taught blond lace.

BOBBIN LACE, BOBBINET, BOBBING, BONE, OR PILLOW LACE, : Eighteenth-century names for bobbin lace. This technique required no needle. Instead, one stuck pins into a pillow through strategic points of a paper or parchment pattern that was attached to a hard pillow. The worker gradually unwound thread held on bobbins or slender bones around the pins, knotting and interlocking the threads as one followed the pattern to create openwork patterns. Privately and in small shops, eighteenth-century women made money producing this

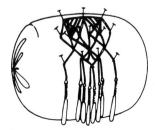

Bobbin lace

Bullion stitch

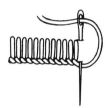

Buttonhole stitch (A)

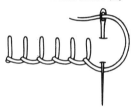

Buttonhole stitch (B)

Buttonhole stitch (C)

lace, especially in Ipswich and Boston, Massachusetts. Miss Ingles, in the *American and Commercial Daily Advertiser* for July 10, 1827, said that besides tuition, it would cost $5.00 more to learn "working on Bobinet, in a style equal to the finest imported laces."

BOLTON, BOUTONNÉ: Today woven coverlets made of a pebbled fabric are called candlewick. Earlier they were known as Bolton, named for a town in Lancashire, England. In French Canada the fabric was known as boutonné. Woven pieces were also made in the mid-Atlantic states and probably in New England. One of the earliest existing woven types is owned by Winterthur Museum and is dated 1773. By the early nineteenth-century embroidered coverlets existed side by side with woven ones, featuring raised loops of soft candlewicking or roving yarn. See KNOTTED COUNTERPAINE for the hand-made type.

BONE LACE: See BOBBIN LACE.

BRODERIE PERSE: A name given in the late nineteenth century to the method of appliqué work in which design elements, such as trees or butterflies, were cut from printed fabrics and sewn to a new background fabric. Usually a blind whip stitch fastened the pieces, although occasionally decorative stitches like the buttonhole, chain, or feather were used. This technique was most popular between 1780 and 1830. Examples: plate 37, figure 128..

BULLION STITCH: An embroidery stitch resembling a tiny wound tube of thread. The embroiderer first took a small stitch and then wrapped the thread around the tip of the needle five to twenty turns before reinserting the needle. Example: plate 24, flower centers, top center.

BUTTONHOLE STITCH: An embroidery stitch with many uses and variations. When worked solidly (A), it resembles the satin stitch, with a tiny twisted edging along one side. Placed on the edge of a buttonhole slit, this edging gives strength. When worked more openly (B), the buttonhole stitch simulates prickers on a stem (Figure 61). (C) Various patterns of detached buttonhole stitches (modern term) were used in CUT WORK,.

CADDOW: The Irish name for loom woven fabric resembling candlewicking.

CANDLEWICKING: A hand embroidered or machine made needlework technique; both methods were popular early in the nineteenth century. In either method the principal decoration was raised stitches of soft candlewicking or roving yarns. A look at the reverse side quickly reveals any machine-made specimen; it is very neat, lacking knots, loops, and the excess yarn that are found on handmade examples. Handmade candlewick coverlets displayed a variety of stitches, including French knots. whip, cross, satin, and bullion. Sometimes the raised stitches were clipped to form tufted areas. For loom woven candlewicking see BOLTON, CADDOW, and BOUTONNÉ; for hand-made examples, see KNOTTED COUNTERPAINE. Examples: Figures 91 and 92.

CANVAS: A plain-woven cloth of cotton, linen, hemp, wool, silk, etc., which today has sizing for stiffness. Canvas is used as the foundation for evenly stitched designs. The number of warp or weft threads per inch determines the size of the canvas. In the early nineteenth century, the Germans began producing canvases with a colored thread every tenth warp yarn. This helped when counting and transferring Berlin patterns (figure 120). PENELOPE CANVAS was woven with warp and weft yarns in pairs. Nineteenth-century canvases tended to be much coarser than previous ones.

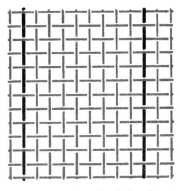

Canvas with colored threads

CANVAS WORK: Used between the seventeenth and nineteenth centuries for the art of filling the square spaces in canvas or other evenly woven background fabric with yarn to make a needleworked design. The yarns used were crewel, silk, or metallic. Another old term sometimes used for canvas work was TAPESTRY WORK. BERLIN WORK became the term for canvas work in the nineteenth century, superseded in the twentieth century by NEEDLEPOINT. Examples: plates 12 and 13.

CATGUT: A term in the eighteenth century for a fine, plain weave of tightly twisted warps and wefts, often used for embroidery. In *the New York Gazette and Weekly Mercury* of May 13, 1765, Isabella Jones said she taught "Dresden flowering on catgut." John and Eleanor Druitt taught, "drawn cat-gut black and white with a Number of beautiful Stitches" according to their advertisement in *The Massachusetts Gazette and Boston Weekly News Letter* of April 4, 1774.

CHAIN STITCH: A centuries-old term for an embroidery stitch worked with a needle. Its appearance resembles that of tambour work.

Chain stitch

CHENILLE: A fuzzy, silk yarn with a silk core. This yarn originated in France, where chenille means caterpillar. It was used in American embroideries, usually only as accents, during the late eighteenth and nineteenth centuries. Sometimes the yarn was actually stitched through the background fabric with a large-eyed needle, but just as often it was couched down in rows with fine silk thread of the same shade. From the mid-nineteenth century on, a chenille yarn with a wire core was occasionally used in Berlin canvas work. Examples: figures 86 and 110.

COATS OF ARMS: Usually designed by professionals in both lozenge (plate 34) and rectangular (figure 52) shapes for school girls to work in various techniques, including quill work, embroidery, and painting on velvet. One of the earliest known examples is a rectangular filigree piece initialed "B S" (for the Benjamin Smith family of Boston) and dated 1693. By the mid-eighteenth century needleworked arms tended to be solidly done in tent stitch on canvas (plate 32). Later in the eighteenth century the background was usually silk fabric, either white or black, with silk embroidered arms (figure 99). An unusual example is an oval design painted on velvet and framed as an octagon (figure 87).

Corded work

CORDED WORK: An eighteenth-century term for a technique also called Marseilles quilting. The needleworker stitched design outlines through two layers of fabric using fine running or back stitches. A soft cording was pulled through the narrow outlined channels from the back of the work, raising the design area on the front. Frequently this technique was combined with stuffed work and flat quilting. The name TRAPUNTO was not applied to American MARSEILLES WORK until the twentieth century. By 1760, machine-made examples imitating cording and stuffed work were imported into America. Example: figure 89.

COTTON-WOOL: Another term for cotton batting. Since the eighteenth century, its primary use was as an interlining for quilts. Quilts made before the cotton gin was perfected usually reveal numerous cotton seeds in the cotton-wool when held to the light. In the *Essex Gazette* (Salem, Massachusetts) for May 11-18, 1773, Francis Grant offered cotton-wool for sale. Example: figure 122.

CREPE WORK: A Moravian needlework form popular after 1818 in Bethlehem, Pennsylvania, and shortly thereafter in Lititz. Strips of sheer silk fabric were folded, gathered, and stitched down for a three-dimensional effect. The whole was then embellished with chenille yarn and fine ribbon work. Example: figure 86.

CREWEL: A word that at least since Shakespeare's time has meant two-ply, slackly twisted, worsted yarns and that has had a variety of spellings: crewil, cruell, cruill, crool, and crewell. Crewel yarns were well known in America and England until Berlin yarns replaced them between 1820 and 1870. Crewel yarns were revived during the late nineteenth-century Art Needlework movement and again in the mid-twentieth century. This yarn may be used for crewel embroidery, knitting, tambour, canvas work, etc. Examples of crewel embroidery: plates 22, 23, 26, and 27. Examples of crewel used for canvas work: plates 12 and 21.

CREWEL EMBROIDERY: A modern term indicating work done with crewel yarns in a variety of stitches, not confined to a canvas or counted-thread foundation.

CREWEL WORK: A modern term indicating any needlework using two-ply, slackly twisted, worsted yarns. The work may be done on a variety of backgrounds: linen, cotton, wool, canvas, or even today's synthetics. Crewel yarn was popular in America for embroidery or canvas work from the last half of the seventeenth century through the eighteenth century. It was revived in the 1870s and again in the 1950s.

CROCHET WORK: A series of chain stitches looped into each other by means of a hooked tool. It was related to tambour work, for both require a hook to create the chain stitch. In crochet work, however, the stitch is not held down to a background fabric, as in tambour work. For this reason the French, who originated crochet work, called it "crochet en l'air." The technique spread to Ireland and was brought to the United States in the 1840s by immigrants. Instructions on crocheting appeared in *The Ladies' Work-Table Book*, published in Philadelphia in 1847.

CROSS STITCH: A style of stitch used for centuries for embroidery and canvas work. Since it was also the predominant stitch for marking clothing, household linens, and samplers (A), it was frequently called the MARKING STITCH (figure 2 and 24). Although used in America for canvas work in the eighteenth century (plate 17), cross stitch was far more popular for BERLIN WORK (B) in the nineteenth century. It was also called gros point in Berlin work when it crossed several pairs of canvas threads. Also see DOUBLE CROSS STITCH.

Crochet work

Cross stitch (A)

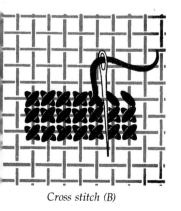

Cross stitch (B)

CUT WORK: A method of making needle lace. An area of the background fabric was completely removed, its raw edges were secured with a holding stitch, and the empty section was filled with detached BUTTONHOLE STITCH. Another contemporary name for this technique was POINTING. An early advertisement was that of Martha Logan in the *South Carolina Gazette* of March 27-April 3, 1742. She taught "plain Work, Embroidery, tent and cut Work." By 1754, the same Martha Logan also advertised Dresden work. The HOLLIE STITCH or HOLLIE POINT were terms used later in the nineteenth century for this work. Examples: figures 23, 75, and 76.

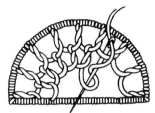

Cut work

DARNING SAMPLERS: Practice pieces designed to teach mending techniques. The needleworker tried to simulate different fabric weaves. Some samplers had deliberate tears or cuts, which were to be repaired. Darning was occasionally mentioned in advertisements, such as *Rivington's New York Gazeteer* listing for February 23, 1775, where an unidentified woman wanted a position teaching "plain Work, Darning, Marking, and Grafting." Example: figure 31.

DARNING STITCH: Also called RUNNING STITCH, it consists of small stitches, equally spaced.

Darning sampler

DIMITY: Originally dimity was not the sheer fabric it is today. FUSTIAN and dimity were sometimes confused. Webster's 1806 *Compendious Dictionary* defined dimity as "a kind of white fustian, a fine fustian." Although dimity and fustian were both used in American crewel work, plain-woven linen backgrounds predominate. Examples: figures 56 and 57.

DOUBLE CROSS STITCH: The name used in the eighteenth century for a cross stitch which made a cross over four threads, then a smaller cross over two threads, each arm in the opposite direction. Usually used for carpets or upholstery. In England, Mrs. Delany said, "My candlelight work is finishing a carpet in double cross stitch on very coarse canvas to go round my bed" (quoted in Therle Hughs, *English Domestic Needlework, 1660-1860,* London, 1961, page 50). Modern terms for this stitch are rice stitch and crossed corners.

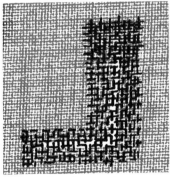

Darning sampler

DRAWN WORK: See DRESDEN WORK.

DRESDEN WORK: The surviving examples of American Dresden work were done on a sheer, plain woven linen often called tiffany. (A) Areas to be worked are outlined in chain, satin, or buttonhole stitches. In these areas threads are counted and drawn together with stitches into various patterns. Sometimes the different petals of a single flower will have different patterns (Example: the tulip-like flower in the center of figure 76). Elinor and Mary Purcell were early advertisers of the technique, offering, "Dresden on Lawn and Muslin" in the *The Boston Evening Post* for May 13, 1751. It had several other names in the eighteenth century. In the January 3, 1771, edition of the *Pennsylvania Gazette,* Lucy Brown and Ann Ball announced, "Sisters, Natives of England lately arrived from Paris [would teach] weave lace." Mrs. Anderson, in the *Pennsylvania Gazette* for April 12, 1759, used a rare term, BERLIN NEEDLEWORK: "all Manner of Berlin or Dresden NEEDLEWORK." (Berlin work, the canvas-work technique of the nineteenth century, was not yet in use.) Dresden work was called drawn work increasingly during the nineteenth century. (B) Certain linen threads are removed completely and needlework stitches are added to decorate the remaining warp threads by grouping them

Double cross stitch

Dresden work

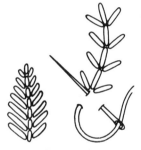

Feather stitch

Fern stitch

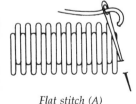

Flat stitch (A)

Flat stitch reverse (A)

together in a pattern. This method was often used to decorate Pennsylvania hand towels (figure 74).

ECONOMY STITCH: See FLAT STITCH.

FAMILY REGISTER: Another eighteenth- and nineteenth- century name for GENEALOGICAL SAMPLERS. Example: plate 8.

FANCY WORK: Until at least the mid-nineteenth century, this term included all the embroidery and CANVAS WORK stitches and techniques. Except for women who had been trained as professional embroiderers, only those with leisure time and a needlework education practiced fancywork. To do fancywork, therefore, implied that the needleworker had attained a certain level of social stature and accomplishment.

FEATHER STITCH: One of the few embroidery stitches specifically named in an American newspaper advertisement. Eleanor Druitt in the *Boston Gazette* for March 21, 1774, said she taught "Feather-Stitch" along with an extensive list of other popular techniques. It was a novelty that Mrs. Druitt advertised because American embroidery of the eighteenth century rarely contained the feather stitch.

FERN STITCH: One of the names mentioned in John Taylor's 1640 poem "In Praise of the Needle." In American embroidery, the major use of it was to stitch the foliage of weeping willow trees in mourning pictures. Example: figure 116.

FLAME STITCH: A twentieth-century name for the IRISH STITCH used for CANVAS WORK.

FLAT QUILTING: A decorative, rather than utilitarian, style of quilting that used two layers of fabric and had no interlining. This allowed the needleworker to do even finer quilting stitches than on quilts of three layers, sometimes gathering areas slightly to form puckering. Popular in England, flat quilting was most often used in America to decorate the smooth areas of stuffed and corded pieces.

FLAT STITCH: A stitch often found in solidly worked areas of American crewelwork. Originally this name may have stood for two different stitches. Both techniques resemble satin stitch and cover the area solidly on the front, but unlike satin stitch, both have only small vertical stitches on the back.

(A) The point of the needle goes up a small stitch before the top line and creates a smoother effect, but is slower to work. In a variation of this, the needle goes down a small stitch from the top line.

(B) A small stitch is taken over the top of each long one after it is worked. Its appearance is not as smooth as satin stitch because of this extra stitch. The reverse side shows only small stitches.

Embroiderers seem to have used both A and B indiscriminately as both can be found on a single piece of work and even in the same area. On November 1, 1753 Joseph Garton, an engraver from the West Indies, advertised in the *Maryland Gazette* that he, "undertakes all manner of Engraving in the Flat Stitch Way on Silver or Gold Plate." Modern names for this stitch are Roumanian couching, Oriental, New England laid, economy, overlaid, and Roman. Example: figure 55.

Flat stitch (B)

Flat stitch reverse (B)

FLORENTINE STITCH: A term that first appeared in American needlework books late in the nineteenth century to replace the earlier term IRISH STITCH.

FRENCH KNOT: An embroidery stitch that creates a tiny, circular knot. Small areas of closely set French knots formed an interesting texture and were often used on CANVAS WORK and embroidery to form flower centers or sheep's wool.

FUSTIAN: Fustian was a twill-woven fabric, usually of a cotton weft on a linen warp but occasionally all cotton. Surviving early CREWEL WORK and early written references show a preference for backgrounds of either fustian or DIMITY.

French knots

GENEALOGICAL SAMPLER: A needlework piece that lists the members of a family in chart form, or more ingeniously, as fruit on a family tree. Samplers which mentioned a few family members have existed from at least 1725; however, the true genealogical samplers were particularly fashionable from 1790 to 1835. Example: plate 8.

GERMAN CANVAS: A canvas usually made of cotton. Every tenth warp yarn was colored to help when counting and transferring Berlin patterns. Example: figure 120.

GERMAN YARN: See BERLIN YARN.

HATCHMENTS: Family or pseudo family arms, usually painted on wood or carved in stone in a lozenge shape. These were placed on a casket or in a church. In his 1806 *Compendious Dictionary*, Noah Webster called hatchments "escutcheon set up for the dead." This custom was practiced much more in Europe and England than in America. Silversmiths in America frequently owned heraldry books (Paul Revere is leaning on one in his John Singleton Copley portrait) and offered to provide arms for silver or for needlework. Compare with COATS OF ARMS.

HERRINGBONE STITCH: Known by this name as early as the eighteenth century, it is a loosely worked embroidery stitch, resembling a lattice. More recent names and variations are ladder, shadow, long-armed cross, or mossoul cross-stitch.

Herringbone stitch

HOLLIE STITCH, HOLLIE POINT: See CUT WORK.

HUNGARIAN STITCH, POINT D'HONGRIE: Names used in American needlework books only after the late nineteenth and twentieth centuries as a substitute for the earlier term IRISH STITCH. Point d'Hongrie in the early eighteenth century referred to a very coarse French fabric woven on a loom in a zigzag design and used to cover the cold stone walls of castles.

Unfortunately, this fabric is now often considered needlework and is used to cover antique easy chairs and other furniture.

INLAID WORK: A rare variation of APPLIQUÉ QUILTING, practiced from the middle of the eighteenth century to early in the nineteenth century. Today it is sometimes called REVERSE APPLIQUÉ. The quilter cut her design out of the background fabric, turned the edges under to prevent raveling, then laid colored fabrics under the open areas, and stitched both layers together. In the *Georgia Gazette* (Savannah) of November 2, 1774, William Obryen offered forty shillings as reward for *"A BED QUILT"* stolen from his bed, which had in "the middle [a] large tree (inlaid work) with a peacock at the root and five small birds on the branches."

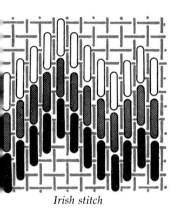

Irish stitch

IRISH STITCH: More surviving examples of eighteenth-century American canvas work were done in the Irish stitch than in any other technique. It was fast-moving, the vertical stitches progressing four threads at a time. From the early seventeenth century until the 1880s, it was known in England and America by this name. Then it began to be called the FLORENTINE and gradually, BARGELLO, HUNGARIAN, and FLAME STITCH. Mrs. Wright in the *South Carolina Gazette* (Charleston) of July 13-20, 1747, advertised that she taught the Irish stitch. Examples: plates 11, 13, 16; figure 48.

KNITTING: An ancient method of making a stretchable fabric with a single length of yarn. Using two or more narrow, long pins as needles, the knitter looped yarn in a way so as to form a series of interlocked stitches in vertical rows. Some women knit elaborate stitches, mixed yarn colors, or even knitted lace. Example: plate 20; figure 7.

KNOTTED COUNTERPAINE: Four "fashionable knotted counterpanes for bed" and another "white knotted counterpaine" were listed in the inventory of Charles Carroll of Carrollton, Maryland, on October 17, 1806. This was an early reference to the hand-made coverlets we call CANDLEWICK today. These often feature a variety of embroidery stitches such as French knots, whip, chain, and satin. Sometimes the raised stitches were clipped to form domed, tufted areas. A quick look at the back of an embroidered piece reveals knots, loops, and stretched threads instead of the neat back of the loomed variety. See BOLTON for the loom woven type. Examples: figures 91 and 92.

KNOTTING: In this technique the worker used a pointed oval shuttle wound with wool, silk, or linen thread. By forming knots at close, regular intervals, a strand of knotted yarn was formed. These strands would then be stitched down in single or multiple rows as trimming. In figure 1, the woman is knotting as she walks.

MAP SAMPLER: Produced in limited numbers in the United States; more popular in England. The art teacher James Cox advertised in the *Pennsylvania Packet* for September 2, 1790, that he accurately copied "Copperplate Prints, Maps and Paintings" for needlework. Examples: figures 29 and 30.

MARKING: The common term for adding an identifying device, letter, or number on fabric articles. Alphabets and numbers were worked (usually in the CROSS, or MARKING, STITCH) on simple samplers as patterns to be referred to for marking clothing and household linens. Example: figures 18, 88, and 89.

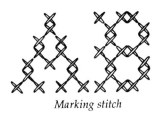

Marking stitch

MARKING STITCH: See CROSS STITCH.

MARSEILLES QUILTING: In the eighteenth century, this term included two different techniques. Advertisements show that before 1760 it was an entirely hand-made product which resembled today's stuffed or corded work. The *South Carolina Gazette* for December 25–January 1, 1750 announced that Mary Irwin and Abraham Varnod "draw for Marseilles quilting." The term French Quilting probably also refers to this work. Both the hand made and early loom made products originated in Marseilles, France. By 1760, the loom made product was imported to America. Both types remained popular until about 1830 when the loom woven variety, made on the Jacquard loom, dominated. Its popularity continued into the twentieth century. Examples of handmade: Figures 89 and 90.

MERINO YARN: See BERLIN YARN.

METALLIC THREADS, METALLIC YARNS: (A) Yarn made with very thinly drawn gold, silver, or brass wire usually wound around a core of silk thread. Example: plate 7. (B) Only rarely used in America was a thin, flat metal thread, without a core. Example: plate 9.

NEEDLE-LACE WORK: Any form of lace made with a needle and thread as opposed to a BOBBIN. Teacher Ruth Hern used the term in the *Boston News-Letter* for March 9, 1775. She probably meant that she taught both CUT WORK and DRESDEN WORK. Example: figure 23.

NEEDLEPOINT: Essentially a twentieth-century term used as a substitute for the earlier contemporary term CANVAS WORK. Today NEEDLEPOINT may also occasionally indicate the popular TENT STITCH.

NET: Before the nineteenth century, the term indicated a finely meshed fabric made by a needle or pillow-lace technique. Machinery for making net was developed early in the nineteenth century. Net, either hand or machine made, was the foundation fabric for NETTED LACE. Sarah Hays in the June 9, 1768, *Pennsylvania Gazette*, advertised that she taught net work. Example: center of white embroidery: figure 78.

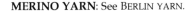

Netted lace

NETTED LACE: A form that required a foundation of hand- or machine-made net. The needle woman then used embroidery stitches to fill in some of the meshes to form lace-like designs.

NETTING: A technique that produced both very fine netted lace and very coarse fish nets.. A netting needle was a long, slim rod with a slit at each end to wind the thread. After fastening the first loop to something firm, the rest of the stitches or loops were built on it by knotting the thread at regular intervals. While the knots were being formed, different-sized gauges (bone or ivory sticks) were held as the meshes were formed so that the holes would all be of a uniform size. This work was used for trimming. Example: figure 78.

ONE-PIECE QUILTS: Those quilts in which the top layer was a single fabric (or several widths sewn together, as opposed to pieced or appliquéed tops). They were most popular during the eighteenth century. Since they had no other decoration, one-piece quilts characteristically had elaborate quilted designs worked in fine running or backstitches. Examples: figures 10, 11, 123, and 124.

ORIENTAL STITCH: See FLAT STITCH.

OUTLINE STITCH: See WHIP STITCH.

PAPER EMBROIDERY: A few surviving pictures were stitched in silk on paper backgrounds in America. Sarah Mangles said in the *Pennsylvania Gazette* of October 11, 1786, that she taught, "needle-work in silk and worsted, tambour and paper." Existing examples are worked over drawings or copperplate prints. Those examined by the author show surface satin stitch and French knots. Because of the skill involved, perhaps these pieces were tests of the students' abilities.

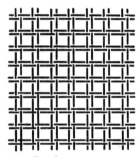
Penelope canvas

PATCHES: Pieces of printed fabrics, often used for making appliquéed quilts. Rebecca Amory in *The Boston Evening Post* for October 10, 1763, said she had "English & India Patches" for sale. The scene around the tree trunk in figure 127 is from an English roller printed fabric.

PATCHWORK: An eighteenth- and nineteenth-century term apparently used indiscriminately to describe the pieced or appliquéed techniques. In the 1782 Baltimore County probate record of James Kingsbury is listed "1 Counterpin patch work—45 shillings."

PENELOPE CANVAS: Canvas woven with paired warp and weft yarns. Developed about 1840, it allowed the needle woman to more easily see the canvas if she used the paired threads as a single unit. Or she could separate the paired threads and work specific areas four times as finely. Mention and a drawing of penelope canvas in a description of an antimacassar appear in the May, 1849, issue of *Godeys Lady's Magazine and Lady's Book,* page 362.

PETIT POINT: A French term, used only rarely in eighteenth-century America, that began to appear in nineteenth-century sewing books to mean the TENT STITCH. The tent, or petit point, stitch crossed one or two intersections of the threads of the canvas diagonally. At times, especially in the twentieth century, the term also indicates work done on today's finest canvas.

PIECED WORK, PIECED QUILTS: Nineteenth-century terms that referred to constructing a piece of fabric by stitching together smaller pieces of different fabrics. Joining straight-edged pieces, and making them lie flat, was far easier than using curved pieces (figure 130). When the needleworker added a lining and interlining and stitched through the three layers, it became a pieced quilt. Examples: figures 125 and 126.

PILLOW LACE: See BOBBIN LACE.

PLAIN SEWING: Until at least the mid-nineteenth century, this term meant stitching seams, hems, buttonholes and marking clothing and household linens; it usually also included knitting. Example: figure 2.

POINTING: See CUT WORK.

PRINT WORK: In needlework, the technique of using very tiny black stitches to imitate the engraved or stippled lines of a copperplate print. A favorite engraving was traced (usually by a professional) onto the silk background. A good contemporary description of a print work was given in a review of the Second Annual exhibition of the Society of Artists in the *Port Folio* of August, 1812. An entry exhibited by Mrs. Eddowes was described as "a piece of needle work in imitation of engraving in the line manner—worked on white satin with black silk, the threads of which appear like the lines of engraving." Needlework books in the 1850s were still describing this technique. Example: the center area of figure 43.

Queen's stitch

QUEEN'S STITCH: The most complex of all canvas-work stitches. Each unit was made up of four or five stitches crossed in the center by a tiny horizontal stitch. Because of so many stitches entering one square, holes were formed at the top and bottom of the stitch, giving a characteristic texture to the Queen's stitch. Usually worked only in silk, this stitch was so time-consuming that it was commonly confined to small items. Elizabeth Drinker mentioned in October of 1758 that she "finish'd a Queen's stitch Pocket Book." The height of the limited vogue of the Queen's stitch seems to have been between 1780 and 1810. It has been almost totally neglected since then, although some needlework books continued to show it. Late in the nineteenth century, the name gradually changed to ROCOCO STITCH. Example: figure 49.

QUILLING: Narrow strips (about one-quarter inch) of colored paper were purchased to make various shapes, including flat rolls, cones, or mounds. The individual shapes were then glued down to form flowers, animals, buildings, and scenes. Some also had dressed dolls, carved animals, and shells to form a picture. The finished composition was usually sprinkled with mica, set off in a deep frame and often with an attached candle arm below the frame to light the picture and enhance the sparkle. Example: figure 42.

QUILTING: The process of fastening three layers of fabric together, usually with running, back, or machine stitching. The top layer may have embroidery, piecing, or appliqué decoration applied before being quilted. But in the so-called ONE-PIECE QUILT, the quilting stitches themselves were the only decoration. During the Victorian era, spaced ties, or tufting, sometimes substituted for stitching. Examples: one-piece quilt, figure 124; pieced quilt, figure 126; appliquéed quilt, figure 130.

QUILTS: Warm bed coverings made from three layers of fabric: a top piece most commonly of cotton, wool, linsey-woolsey, or silk; an interlining, of cotton-wool, woven wool, or eider down; and the lining, of cotton, silk, linen, linsey-woolsey, or wool. The needle woman stitched through these three layers, creating various designs. Besides being made in the home, quilts were professionally quilted. or imported ready-made. On November 25, 1776, Elizabeth Evans advertised in the *New, York Gazette and Weekly Mercury* that she "wrought quilts."

RAISED WORK: A general term used for any needlework with artificially raised areas. Carved wood, molded clay, and fiber or fabric fillings were used underneath to shape a figure. Then it was covered with fabric and decorated. MARSEILLES, or corded, work was also considered raised work.

RIBBON WORK: A form that used specially shaded and dyed narrow silk ribbons instead of yarn or thread to work embroidery designs, and especially tiny flowers. Apparently Moravian schools introduced this needlework form from Europe about 1818. Although seldom worked later in the nineteenth century, ribbon work was given a new name in Victorian needlework books: rococo work. Example: figure 38.

RICE STITCH: See DOUBLE CROSS STITCH.

ROCOCO STITCH: A mid- to late-nineteenth-century name for the QUEEN'S STITCH used in CANVAS WORK.

Running stitch

RUNNING STITCH: Small, straight stitches evenly spaced. Basic to plain sewing for seaming, darning, quilting, and gathering areas, it was also an early decorative stitch when varied slightly. One variation, used for early black work, required a second running stitch to follow the first, filling in the original spaces. Another variation was used for many bed rugs, on which a raised loop was formed by not pulling the yarn flat on the material. Example: figures 11 and 63.

SAMPLER: A needlework form recording stitches and designs, usually but not always signed and dated. Samplers functioned variously over time as reference works and as statements of ability. Also called sams or examplars. American ones survive from as early as the mid-seventeenth century. Examples: plate 6; figures 17, 19, 20–26, 31, 35, 36.

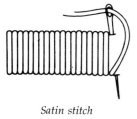

Satin stitch

SATIN STITCH: An embroidery stitch that is useful for covering areas solidly. The stitch, worked in a compact fashion, uses as much yarn on the back as on the front. It is possible to work the satin stitch so neatly that the back appears almost identical to the front. In American crewelwork, this stitch was rarely used except to fill small accent areas. Compare to SURFACE SATIN STITCH and WHIP STITCH.

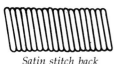

Satin stitch back

SATIN STITCH PICTURES: A modern term for needlework especially popular between 1785 and 1840, executed with silk yarns, usually on silk backgrounds. Silk work was done earlier but was far less common (plates 5 and 7). Philadelphia's Mrs. Mallon, in her May 11, 1802, advertisement in *The Aurora General Advertiser*, listed the typical subjects as "Figure Flower, and Landscape Embroidery." Miss Lambert's 1851 *Hand-Book of Needlework*, page 87, describes her method of tracing a design "for embroidering in satin-stitch." Ironically, some of the very large solid areas of these pictures only appear to be satin stitched, for when looked at from the back of the piece, they are seen as compact rows of WHIP STITCH. FRENCH KNOTS and SEED STITCH were often used as accents. Examples: plate 36; figure 101.

SEED OR SEEDING STITCH: A term used since early in the eighteenth century to describe groups of tiny stitches that resemble random dots, often used to fill flower centers.

Seed stitch

SHINING STITCH: See FLAT STITCH and SATIN STITCH.

SPANGLES: The eighteenth-century term for sequins, made of tiny silver, gold, copper, and brass disks. An early reference to their use appeared in Mrs. Cole's advertisement in the *New York Gazette and Weekly Mercury* for April 4, 1774, saying that she would teach each person "to spangle." Spangles became most popular in the years from 1800 to 1840. Example: figure 100.

STEM STITCH: A modern name for WHIP STITCH.

Spangles

STUFFED WORK: See RAISED WORK.

SURFACE SATIN STITCH: A stitch that is almost impossible to distinguish on the front from a true SATIN STITCH. However, each time the needle goes to the back of the work it is returned to the front next to the previous exit hole. The back thus appears to have two parallel lines of fine running stitches. Examples: plates 5 and 7.

TAMBOUR WORK: A needlework form that derived its name from the drum-shaped frame (plate 10) used to stretch the fabric. Instead of a needle, a tiny hook (figure 79) drew a loop of thread from below the fabric to the surface. Reinserting the hook and repeating this operation produced a chain stitch much faster than using a needle. The technique probably originated in India, where a frame was not used. The French introduced the frame as well as the name. Perhaps the earliest to mention this work in America was Mrs. Bontamps, a French emigre milliner, in the *Pennsylvania Gazette* for December 29, 1768, saying, "She also embroiders in gold, Silver, Silk and Thread, upon the late invented Tambour." The height of tambour's popularity occurred just before the end of the eighteenth century and during the early years of the nineteenth. Example: figure 79.

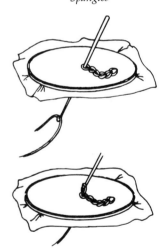

Tambour work

TAPESTRY WORK: Either loom made or hand stitched canvas work. The latter often attempted to imitate the former, inspired by the output of the Gobelin factory in France. In the July 19-28, 1739, *South Carolina Gazette* (Charleston), Jane Voyer mentions several forms she taught, including "Tapistry or any other sort of Needle-work."

TATTING: A process by which a pointed oval shuttle, instead of a needle, creates work similar to lace. The shuttle's thread is knotted into a series of loops around the fingers. During the eighteenth century, tatting was practiced in Europe more than in America.

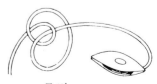

Tatting

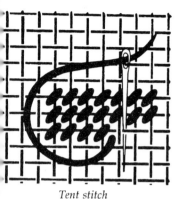

Tent stitch

Whip stitch

TENT STITCH: Also spelled ten or tenth. It meant a canvas-work stitch that diagonally crossed every one or two intersections of threads of the background. The tent stitch, a popular and very old stitch, was especially useful on fine canvases for producing intricate designs and scenes. Teachers like Martha Logan in the *South Carolina Gazette* (Charleston) of August 1-8, 1754, specifically mentioned, "all kinds of Tent and Dresden Work." Before the twentieth century the stitch was worked back and forth in either horizontal or vertical rows, which often pulled the background badly out of shape. Examples: plate 12; figures 24 and 25.

THREAD LACE: An eighteenth-century term for BOBBIN LACE made with linen thread.

TIFFANY: A very fine plain woven fabric, usually of linen in America, used as a ground on many Philadelphia and Lancaster samplers, especially those associated with teachers Ann Marsh (figures 103 and 104), Mrs. Galligher, Mrs. Armstrong (figures 105 and 106), and later Mrs. Maguire in Harrisburg and her imitators. Tiffany was also used as a ground for the finest embroidered lace samplers (figures 75, 76, and 77).

TRAPUNTO: A term applied in the twentieth century to American and English stuffed and corded work.

WEAVE LACE: See DRESDEN WORK.

WHIP STITCH: The name of a common embroidery stitch. The Englishman John Taylor in his 1640 poem "In Praise of the Needle" mentioned this name, which was used continuously into the nineteenth century. More modern names are the outline, stem, stalk, crewel, and rope. When the right side of the whip stitch is stretched out and worked in compact rows, it can appear as a slightly slanting SATIN STITCH. The back has a series of shorter, spaced slanting stitches. Example: figures 100 and 106.

WHITE WORK: An early generic term for several techniques popular in the late seventeenth through early nineteenth centuries and worked on white fabrics with white yarns. Examples: cutwork, figure 9; knotted counterpaine, figures 90 and 91; lace, figure 75; network figure 77; raised and corded work, figure 88; tambour and lace, figure 79.

ZEPHYR YARN: See BERLIN YARN.

BIBLIOGRAPHY

DMMC, WM = Joseph Downs
Manuscript and Microfilm Collection,
Henry Francis du Pont Winterthur
Museum Libraries.

MAGAZINES, NEWSPAPERS, AND MISCELLANEOUS DOCUMENTS

Baltimore American and Commercial Daily Advertiser, 1827.
Boston Evening-Post, 1739.
The Boston Magazine, 1784.
The Georgia Gazette, 1774.
Godey Lady's Book.
Miss Leslie's Magazine.
New York Mercury, 1754, 1756, 1758, 1766.
Pennsylvania Gazette, 1767, 1768, 1813.
Pennsylvania Ledger and Weekly Advertiser, 1775.
Pennsylvania Packet, 1774.
Rivington's New York Gazeteer, 1774.
South Carolina Gazette, 1740, 1753, 1772, 1774.
Watts, Rev. Isaac. *Divine Songs for Children.*
Webster, Daniel. *Compendious Dictionary*, 1806.

MANUSCRIPTS AND UNPUBLISHED SOURCES

Account of Betsey Dorsey, teacher's folder, Maria Rosina Schulze, 1750-1817, Moravian Archives, Bethlehem, Pa.
Accounts of the school, John G. Kummer, Moravian Archives, Bethlehem, Pa.
Cadwalader Collection, General John Cadwalader, Box 2, Historical Society of Pennsylvania, Philadelphia.
Observations sur les Moeurs &c. des Habians de distric à Maine ecrit à New Glocester, 1797. DMMC, WM, no. 61x69.
Diary of Elizabeth Drinker, Historical Society of Pennsylvania, Philadelphia, Pa.
Diary of Mehetable May Dawes, Schlesinger Library, Radcliffe College, Cambridge, Mass.
Indenture of Sarah Wade. DMMC, WM, 76x98.117.
Inventory of John Turner, Probate Records of Sturbridge, Mass., Worcester County. DMMC, WM, (Ph470).
Inventory of Susan Ward, Dorchester, Mass. DMMC, WM, 66x20.
Journal of Esther Burr, Beinecke Rare Book and Manuscript Library, Yale University Library, New Haven, Conn.
Letter of Margaretta Akerly, March 23, 1796, Letters, c. 1796–1801. The New York Historical Society.
Letters of Olney Winsor, 1786-1788. Virginia State Library, Richmond, Va.
Manuscript diary of Hannah Rogers, DMMC, WM, 76x113.
Manuscript diary of Mary S. Steen. Collection of George J. Fistrovich.
Will of John Morris of Southwark, Philadelphia County Probate, 1782, no. 71. DMMC, WM, M1049.

PRIMARY SOURCES

Adams, John and Abigail Smith Adams. *Familiar Letters of John Adams and His Wife Abigail Adams, During the Revolution, with a Memoir of Mrs. Adams.* Boston: Houghton Mifflin Co., 1875.
Alexander, William. *The History of Women from the Earliest Antiquary to Present Time: Giving an Account of Almost Every Interesting Particular Concerning That Sex Among All Nations, Ancient and Modern*, 2 vols. Philadelphia: J. H. Dobelbower, 1796.
Beecher, Catherine E. *A Treatise on Domestic Economy.* New York: Harper and Brothers, 1848.
Bowne, Eliza Southgate. *A Girl's Life Eighty Years Ago: Selections from the Letters of Eliza Southgate Bowne*, intro. by Clarence Cook. New York: Charles Scribner's Sons, 1888.
Buchan, William. *Advice to Mothers, on the Subject of Their Own Health: and on the Means of Promoting the Health, Strength, and Beauty of Their Offspring.* Philadelphia: John Bioren, 1804.
By a Lady. "On the Supposed Superiority of the Masculine Understanding." *The Universal Asylum and Columbian Magazine* (July, 1791).
Countess of Wilton [Egerton, Mary Margaret]. *The Art of Needle-Work from Earliest Times.* London: Colburn, 1840.
Emery, Sarah Anna. *Reminiscences of a Nonagenarian.* Newburyport, Mass.: William H. Huse and Co., 1879.
[Farfar, Eliza Ware Rotch]. *The Young Lady's Friend, by a Lady.* Boston: American Stationers' Co. and John B. Russell, 1836.
Fenlon, F. *Instructions for the Education of a Daughter*, rev. by Dr. George Hicks. London: Jonah Bowyer, 1707.
Fithian, Philip Vichers. *Journal and Letters of Philip Vickers Fithian 1773-1774.* Charlottesville: University Press of Virginia, 1968.
Franks, Rebecca. "Letter of Miss Rebecca Franks." *The Pennsylvania Magazine of History and Biography*, 23 (no. 3, 1899).
Gilman, Mrs. Caroline. *Recollections of a Housekeeper.* New York: Harper and Co., 1834.
Gregory, John. "Gregory's Legacy to his Daughters." *The Lady's Pocket Library* (Philadelphia, Mathew Carey, 1792).
[Hale, Sarah Josepha]. "Advice to a Bride, By a Lady." *The Lady's Book* (May, 1832).
Hamilton, Dr., Alexander. *Outlines of the Theory and Practice of Midwifery*, 3rd American ed. Northhampton: Thomas Andres and Penneman, 1797.
Hopkinson, Joseph. "Address to Pennsylvania Academy of Fine Arts." *The Port Folio* (December, 1810).
"Inventory of Elizabeth Brunson, April 26, 1694." *Early Connecticut Probate Records*, vol. 5 (Hartford: Charles William Manwaring Co., R. S. Peck and Co., 1904).

[Kenrick, William]. *The Whole Duty of a Woman . . . by a Lady. Written at the Desire of a Noble Lord.* Exeter: Stearns and Winslow, 1794.

L. C. "The Ladies of Philadelphia." *Port Folio* IV (no. 6, 1810).

"Letter from a Brother to a Sister at a Boarding School." *Ladies Magazine* (November, 1792).

Livingston, Anne Holme. *Nancy Shippen: Her Journal,* ed. and compiled by Ethel Armes. Philadelphia: J. B. Lippincott Co., 1935.

Mather, Cotton. *Diary of Cotton Mather,* 2 vols. New York: Frederick Ungar Publishing Co., 1957.

_____. *Elizabeth in her Holy Retirement: An Essay to Prepare a Pious Woman for Her Lying In.* Boston: B. Green, 1710.

Matrimonial Republican. "On Matrimonial Obedience." *Ladies Magazine* (July, 1792).

More, Hannah. *Strictures on the Modern System of Female Education with a View of the Principles and Conduct Prevalent among Women of Rank and Fortune,* 2 vols., 6th ed. London: T. Cadell, Jun., and W. Davies, 1799.

_____. "The Essays for Young Ladies." *The Lady's Pocket Library* (Philadelphia, Mathew Carey, 1792).

Nitidia. "Letter to the Editor." *The Columbian Magazine or Monthly Miscellany . . . ,* vol. 1 (no. 8, 1787).

Pennington, Lady. "An Unfortunate Mother's Advice to her Daughters." *The Lady's Pocket Library* (Philadelphia: Mathew Carey, 1792).

Rush, Benjamin. "Thoughts upon Female Education: Accommodated to the Present State of Society, Manners, and Government of the United States of America." *The Universal Asylum and Columbia Magazine* (April, 1790): 209-213; (May, 1790): 288-292.

Sewall, Samuel. "The Letter-Book of Samuel Sewall." *Collection of Massachusetts Historical Society* 6 (ser. 1, 1886).

Sigourney, Mrs. "The Schoolmistress."

The Token. Boston: S. G. Goodrich and Co., 1830.

Thompson, Hannah. "Letters of Hannah Thomson, 1785–1788." *The Pennsylvania Magazine of History and Biography,* vol. 14 (no. 1, 1890).

"Thoughts on Women." *Ladies Magazine* (August, 1792).

Trollope, Frances. *Domestic Manners of Americans,* vol. 1. London: Whittaker, Treacher and Co., 1832.

Twain, Mark. *The Adventures of Huckleberry Finn.* New York: Charles L. Webster and Co., 1885.

_____. *Life on the Mississippi.* Boston: James R. Osgood and Co., 1883.

Vanderpoel, Emily Noyes, compiler. *Chronicles of a Pioneer School from 1792 to 1833, Being the History of Miss Sarah Pierce and her Litchfield School,* ed. Elizabeth C. Barney Buel. Cambridge: The University Press, 1903.

Verme, Count Francesco dal. *Seeing America and Its Great Men: The Journal and Letters of Count Francesco dal Verme 1783-1784,* ed. and trans. Elizabeth Cometti. Charlottesville: University Press of Virginia, 1969.

"Washington's Household Account Book, 1793–1797." *The Pennsylvania Magazine of History and Biography* 29 (no. 4, 1905).

Watson, John Fanning. *Annals of Philadelphia being a Collection of Memoirs, Anecdotes, & Incidents of the City and its inhabitants from the Days of the Pilgrim Founders . . . To which is added an Appendix, containing Olden Time Researchers and Reminiscences of New York City.* Philadelphia: E. L. Carey and A. Hart, 1830.

Winslow, Anna Green. *Diary of Anna Green Winslow, a Boston Schoolgirl of 1771,* ed. by Alice Morse Earle. Boston and New York: Houghton Mifflin Co., 1894.

Wister, Sally. *Sally Wister's Journal: A True Narrative Being a Quaker Maiden's Account of Her Experiences with Officers of the Continental Army,*

1777-1778, ed. by Albert Cook Myers. Philadelphia: Ferris and Leach, 1902.

Wollstonecraft, Mary. *Vindication of the Rights of Woman: With Strictures on Moral and Political Subjects.* Boston: Peter Edes for Thomas and Andrews, 1792.

Woolson, Abba Goold. *Woman in American Society.* Boston: Roberts Brothers, 1873.

[Wray, Mrs. Mary]. *The Ladies Library, By a Lady,* 2 vols. London: Steele, 1714.

Wright, Frances. *Views of Society and Manners in America.* London: Longman, Hurst, Rees, Orne, and Brown, 1822.

SECONDARY SOURCES

Benes, Peter. "Decorated Family Records from Central Massachusetts, New Hampshire, and Connecticut." *Families and Children* (The Dublin Seminar, 1985).

Calhoun, Arthur. *A Social History of the American Family,* 2 vols. New York: Barnes and Noble, Inc., 1945.

Deutsch, Davida Tenenbaum. "Washington Memorial Prints." *The Magazine Antiques* 111 (no. 2, 1977): 324-331.

_____. "Collector's Notes." *The Magazine Antiques* 128 (no. 9, 1985): 526-527.

_____. "Collector's Notes." *The Magazine Antiques* 130 (no. 4, 1986): 646-647.

_____. "Collector's Notes." *The Magazine Antiques* 137 (no. 3, 1989): 616-624.

Flynt, Suzanne. *Ornamental and Useful Accomplishments: Schoolgirl Education and the Deerfield Academy 1800-1830.* Pocumtuck Valley Memorial Association and Deerfield Academy, 1988.

Harris, Paul S. "Gilbert Stuart and a Portrait of Mrs. Sarah Apthrop Morton," *Winterthur Portfolio* 1.

Herr, Patricia T. "Moravian Schoolgirl Needlework in Lititz, Pennsylvania." *The Magazine Antiques* 154 (no. 2, 1993).

Hutson, James H. "Women in the Era of

the American Revolution." *Quarterly Journal of the Library of Congress* (October, 1975).

Krueger, Glee. "Mary Wright Alsop 1740–1829 and Her Needlework." *The Connecticut Historical Society Bulletin*, vol. 52 (nos. 3–4, 1987).

Lockridge, Kenneth A. *Literacy in Colonial New England: An Enquiry into the Social Context of Literacy in the Early Modern West.* New York: W. W. Norton and Co., Inc. 1974.

Ring, Betty. *Girlhood Embroidery: American Samplers and Pictorial Needlework 1650-1850.* 2 vols. New York: Alfred Knopf 1993.

Schuyler, David Paul. *English and American Cottages, 1795–1855,* unpublished masters thesis. University of Delaware, 1976.

Sicherman, Barbara. "American History." *Signs: Journal of Women in Culture and Society* 1 (1975): 461-486.

Swan, Susan Burrows. "Worked Pocketbooks." *The Magazine Antiques* 107 (no. 2, 1975).

_____. "Recent Discoveries about Philadelphia Samplers." *The Magazine Antiques* 136 (no. 6, 1989).

Van Rensselaer, Mrs. John King [May]. *The Goede Vrouw of Mana-Ha-Ta: At Home and in Society, 1609-1760.* New York: Charles Scribner's Sons, 1898.

Index

V

Valances, 123
Verme, Francesco dal, 69

W

Wade, Sarah, 26, 28
Walking wheel, 19
Ward, Susan, 216
Washington, George, 181, 199
Watson, John Fanning, 89–90, 222
Watts, Isaac, 17
Weave lace, 140
Weavers, 19, 21
Weddings, 94
Westtown School, 65, 67
Whip stitch, 157, 189
Willard, Emma, 79
Winslow, Anna Green, 50
Winsor, Nancy. 61
Wister, Sally, 39, 57
Wollstonecraft, Mary, 171, 181–182, 205
Women in business. 132, 135–137
Women's Rights Convention (1848), 132
Women's rights movement, 132
Wool, 19
Woolson, Abba Goold, 83
Worsted yarn, 107
Wright, Frances, 90, 208

Y

Yarns, 19–21, 214–215

Z

Zephyr yarns, 215